ADDISON-WESLEY

QUEST 2000

EXPLORING MATHEMATICS

AUTHORS

Ricki Wortzman   Lalie Harcourt   Brendan Kelly   Peggy Morrow

Randall I. Charles   David C. Brummett   Carne S. Barnett

CONTRIBUTING AUTHORS

Linda Beatty   Anne Boyd   Fred Crouse   Susan Gordon

Elisabeth Javor   Alma Ramirez   Freddie Lee Renfro   Mary M. Soniat-Thompson

REVISED EDITION

Addison-Wesley Publishers Limited

Don Mills, Ontario • Reading, Massachusetts • Menlo Park, California
New York • Wokingham, England • Amsterdam • Bonn
Sydney • Singapore • Tokyo • Madrid • San Juan • Paris
Seoul • Milan • Mexico City • Taipei

Reviewers/Consultants

Marie Beckberger, Springfield Public School, Mississauga, Ontario
Jan Carruthers, Somerset and District Elementary School, King's County, Nova Scotia
Garry Garbolinsky, Tanner's Crossing School, Minnedosa, Manitoba
Darlene Hayes, King Edward Community School, Winnipeg, Manitoba
Barbara Hunt, Bayview Hill Elementary School, Richmond Hill, Ontario
Rita Janes, Roman Catholic School Board, St. John's, Newfoundland
Karen McClelland, Oak Ridges Public School, Richmond Hill, Ontario
Betty Morris, Edmonton Catholic School District #7, Edmonton, Alberta
Jeanette Mumford, Early Childhood Multicultural Services, Vancouver, B.C.
Evelyn Sawicki, Calgary Roman Catholic Separate School District #1, Calgary, Alberta
Darlene Shandola, Thomas Kidd Elementary School, Richmond, B.C.
Elizabeth Sloane, Dewson Public School, Toronto, Ontario
Denise White, Morrish Public School, Scarborough, Ontario
Elizabeth Wylie, Clark Boulevard Public School, Brampton, Ontario

Technology Advisors

Fred Crouse, Centreville, Nova Scotia; Flick Douglas, North York, Ontario; Cynthia Dunham, Framingham, MA;
Susan Seidman, Toronto, Ontario; Evelyn J. Woldman, Framingham, MA; Diana Nunnaley, Maynard, MA

Editorial Coordination: McClanahan & Company
Editorial Development: Susan Petersiel Berg, Margaret Cameron, Mei Lin Cheung,
Fran Cohen/First Folio Resource Group, Inc., Lynne Gulliver, Louise MacKenzie, Helen Nolan, Mary Reeve

Design: McClanahan & Company
Wycliffe Smith Design Inc.

Cover Design: The Pushpin Group

Canadian Cataloguing in Publication Data

Wortzman, Ricki
        Quest 2000 : exploring mathematics, grade 4,
revised edition: student book

First and third authors in reverse order on
previous ed.
ISBN 0-201-55269-8

1. Mathematics – Juvenile literature. I. Harcourt,
Lalie, 1951– . II. Kelly, B. (Brendan), 1943– .
III. Title.

QA107.K44 1996   510   C95–932757-6

ISBN 0-201-55269-8

This book contains recycled product and is acid free.

Printed and bound in Canada.

9 10 11-ITIB-03 02 01

Table of Contents

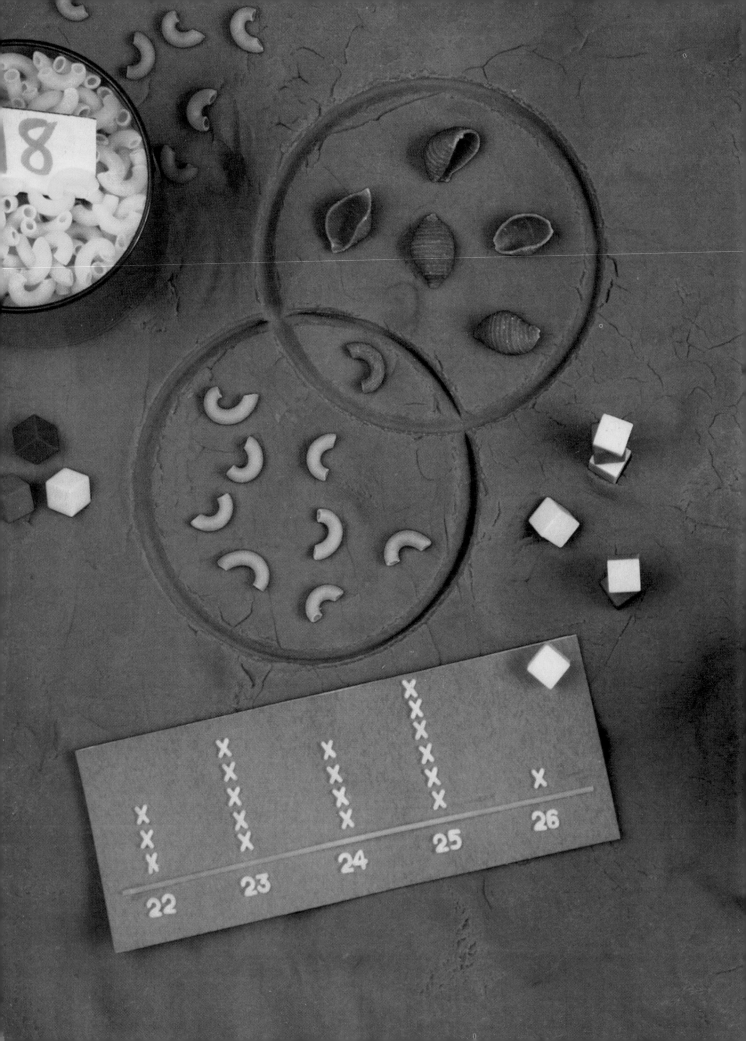

What patterns can we see in data?

COLLECTING AND
ANALYZING DATA

S·T·A·R·T·I·N·G
OUT

LOST AND FOUND

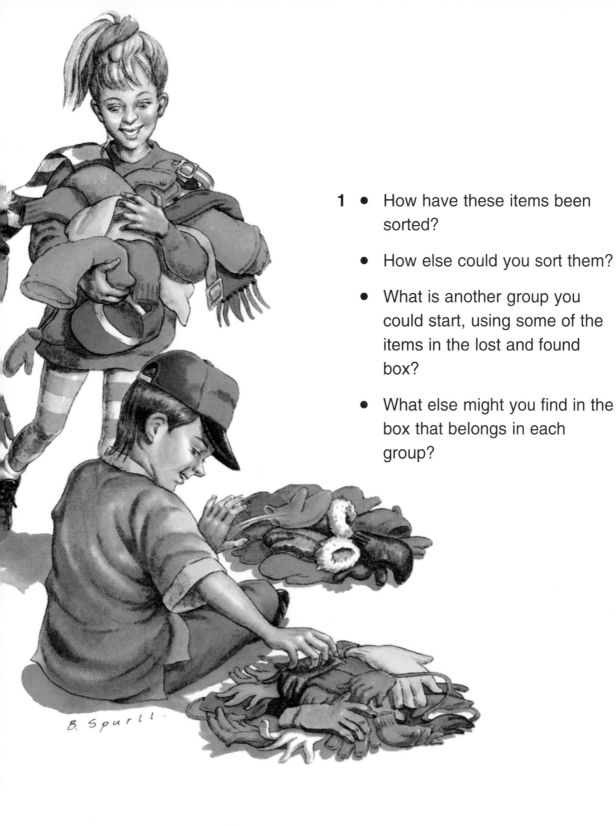

B. Spurll.

1 • How have these items been sorted?

• How else could you sort them?

• What is another group you could start, using some of the items in the lost and found box?

• What else might you find in the box that belongs in each group?

My Journal: When do we sort things? Why is sorting useful?

COLLECTING AND
ANALYZING DATA

S·T·A·R·T·I·N·G
OUT

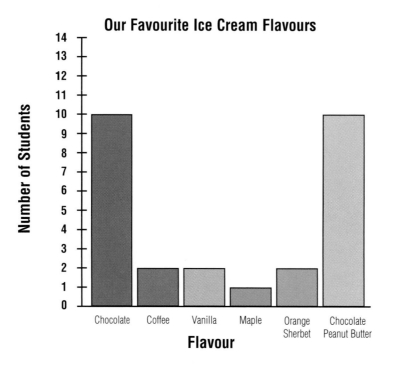

Our Favourite Ice Cream Flavours

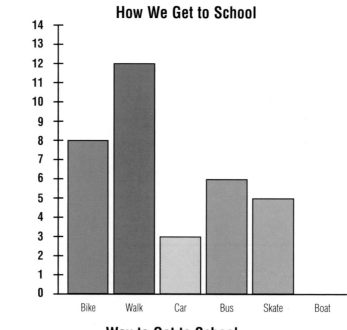

How We Get to School

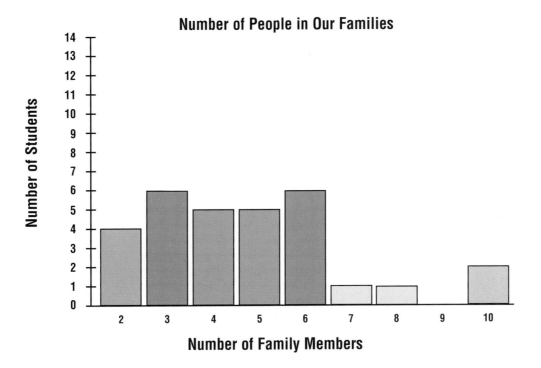

Number of People in Our Families

Number of Students (y-axis, 0–14)

Number of Family Members (x-axis, 2–10)

2 These are graphs for a class of 30 students.

- What do you know about this class from these graphs?

- What else would you like to know about the class?
  How could you find out?

- What explanation can you give as to why the graphs
  don't always show data for exactly 30 people?

- How do you think data from your class would
  compare?

My Journal: How could you find out this information for your own class?

Collecting Data

▶ What data can you
gather about shoes?
Which data need
numbers or measures?
Which data can be
described in other ways?
what ways?

ON YOUR OWN

1. Talk with family members about the characteristics of shoes that are typical in your family. Below are some questions you might ask. Record your family's comments and answers.

   a. What are the characteristics of the most typical shoe you own? Explain.

   b. How can you describe the characteristics of a typical shoe for your family?

   c. What is the typical length of time that a shoe lasts in your family? How can you explain the variations?

   d. Are the characteristics of your favourite shoe typical of your other shoes?

2. *My Journal:* What does "typical" mean to you?

Practise Your Skills

Use the data from the chart.
1. How many pairs of shoes were purchased?
2. Who might have been surveyed for these data?
3. What is the typical cost of the shoes purchased?

Cost of Shoes	Number of Pairs of Shoes Purchased
Up to $10	✔ ✔
$11–$20	✔ ✔ ✔ ✔ ✔
$21–$30	✔ ✔ ✔ ✔ ✔ ✔ ✔ ✔ ✔
$31–$40	✔ ✔
More than $40	✔ ✔ ✔

Examining Data

A line plot can give us a quick picture of numerical data.
▶ Which numbers belong on the line plot?
Which is the greatest number?
Which is the least number?

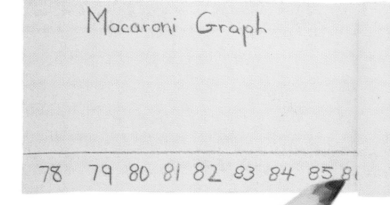

Macaroni Graph

78 79 80 81 82 83 84 85 8(

79

85

96

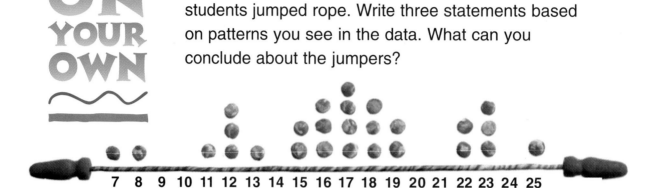

ON YOUR OWN

1. This line plot shows the number of times some Grade 4 students jumped rope. Write three statements based on patterns you see in the data. What can you conclude about the jumpers?

7 8 9 10 11 12 13 14 15 16 17 18 19 20 21 22 23 24 25

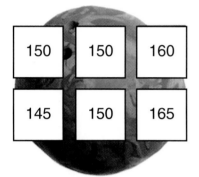

150	150	160
145	150	165

2. Michael bowls three games each week with his bowling club. His scores for five weeks are shown to the left. Show these scores on a line plot. Write five statements you can make about Michael's scores based on the line plot.

3. *My Journal:* What questions do you have about line plots?

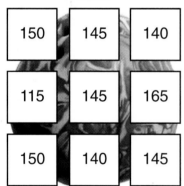

150	145	140
115	145	165
150	140	145

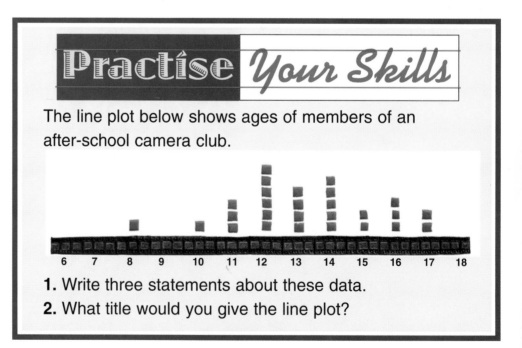

Practise Your Skills

The line plot below shows ages of members of an after-school camera club.

6 7 8 9 10 11 12 13 14 15 16 17 18

1. Write three statements about these data.
2. What title would you give the line plot?

Food for Thought

Have you ever wondered where some of your favourite foods come from?

Take a survey of your class to find out what each person's three favourite foods are. Decide on a way to record your data.

Then work in groups to find out the origins of the three most popular foods in your class.

Yogurt
from the Middle
East (but not
frozen yogurt)

Pizza
origin unclear, but
the ingredients
are Italian!

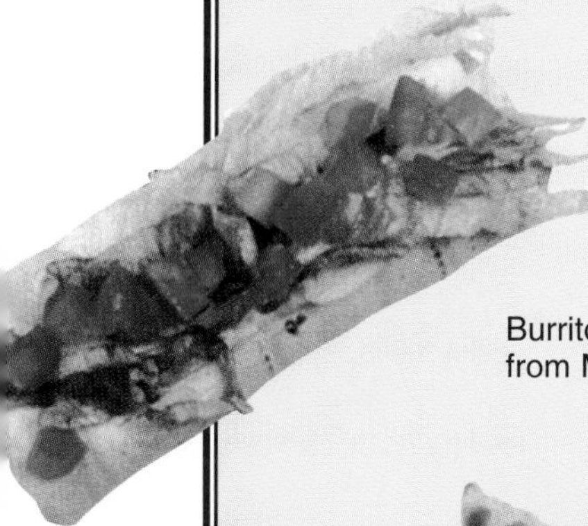

Burrito
from Mexico

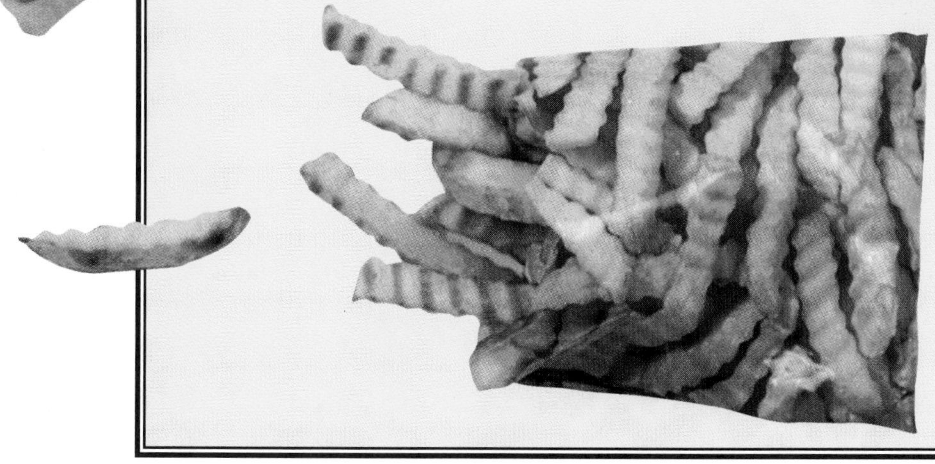

French fries or *frites*
you guess, but the ketchup was
known as far back as 1690 in
China and Malaysia.

Analyzing Data

Directions for Building Towers

1. Use only 1 cube for your base.

2. Your tower cannot lean against anything else.

3. You cannot use tape or anything else to make the cubes stick together.

4. You need to be careful not to shake or bump tables where anyone is working.

Here are data about twelve apartment buildings in one city neighbourhood.

Building	Year Built	Storeys	Apartments	Elevators	Entrances	Exterior
Carlton Arms	1947	10	50	2	2	brick
Kimball Court	1967	4	28	0	4	wood
Heritage Commons	1993	10	20	2	4	brick
The Parkview	1975	7	28	1	4	brick
Holmes House	1982	12	60	2	3	brick
Breezy Point	1959	3	12	0	2	wood
Terrace Gardens	1970	3	15	0	3	wood
A. Muir Coops	1973	12	75	3	4	brick
MacDonald Towers	1990	15	150	5	5	brick
The Ojibwa	1896	10	20	2	5	brick
La Maison	1960	8	32	2	2	brick
San Remo	1925	10	20	2	2	brick

1. Make a separate line plot for each of the categories: number of storeys, number of apartments, number of elevators, and number of entrances.

   Use your line plots and other data in the table to write a description of what a typical building in this neighbourhood is like. Justify your conclusions using the line plot and data table.

2. Who would want to know the characteristics of the most typical building in a neighbourhood? How might they use these data?

3. *My Journal:* What have you learned about line plots?

Exploring Mean

▶ Where should the measurement begin?
Where should it end?
How can you be sure that everyone
measures the same way?
What could you use if you don't have a
tape measure?

1. What is the typical hat size in your family? How can you find out? What data can you record? Try it! Write about what you did, what you found out, and what problems, if any, you faced.

2. What is the average size of an egg? What measure(s) would you take? How many eggs would you examine to answer the question? Try it at home if you can. But be careful – don't drop any eggs as you investigate! If hardboiled eggs are available, use them.

3. Kevin went to Dr. Hsia for his yearly checkup. Dr. Hsia said that Kevin was taller than average. What does this mean?

4. *My Journal:* What have you learned about describing data?

Practise Your Skills

1. Find the number in the middle and the most frequent number.
   12, 13, 13, 13, 15, 18, 18

2. Find the number in the middle and the most frequent number.
   103, 110, 123, 135, 173, 173, 184

3. Round each of these numbers to the nearest ten.
   14, 27, 48, 75, 32

4. Round each of these numbers to the nearest hundred.
   638, 291, 347, 850, 763

True or Not?

Typical Statements

- In 1995, a person in Canada spent about $1.59 on average to buy a dozen eggs.
- A working person saves on average 5¢ out of every dollar he or she earns.
- In Canada, a child (ages 2–11) watches on average $18\frac{1}{2}$ hours of television per week.
- Writers average about 20 words per sentence.
- The mass of an average man is 73 kg.
- A person who leaves the water running while brushing his or her teeth wastes an average of about 27 L of water per week.
- In Canada, a person uses an average of almost 4 kg of paper per week.

Create a statement like the ones on the left about the members of your class. Collect data on the statement, organize the data, and choose a graph to show your results. The data the class collects will help to describe what a "typical" student in your class is like!

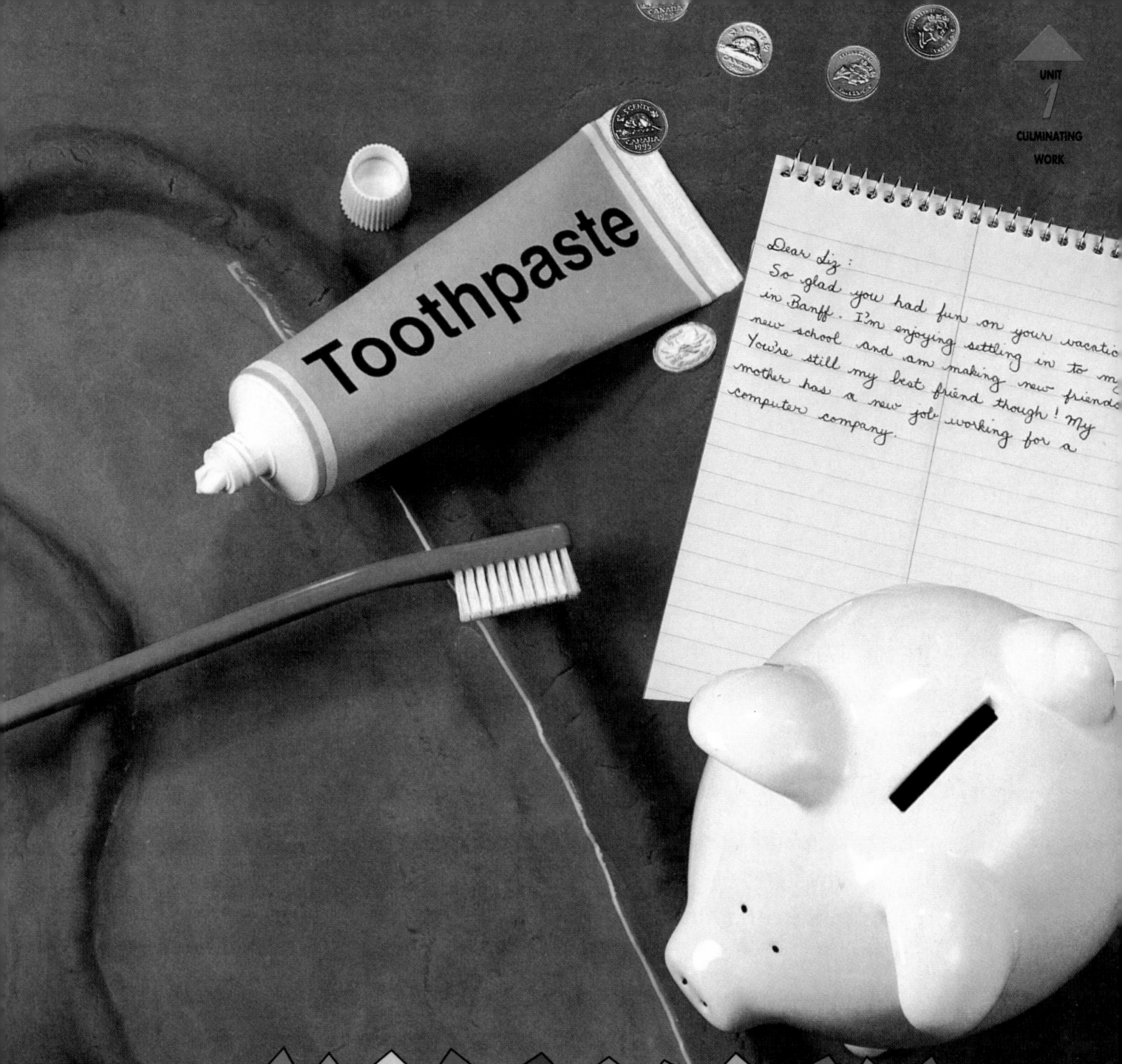

Toothpaste

Dear Liz:
So glad you had fun on your vacatio
in Banff. I'm enjoying settling in to m
new school and am making new friends
You're still my best friend though! My
mother has a new job working for a
computer company.

$\mathcal{C}$heck**Y**OURSELF

Great job! Your data collection is complete and organized. You analyzed it and drew appropriate conclusions about the mean, the median, or the mode, and communicated these clearly in writing.

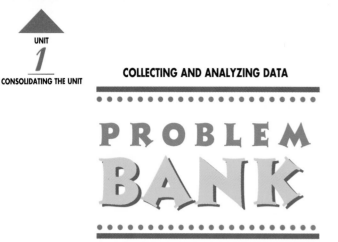

PROBLEM BANK

1. Rosa and Fred surveyed some friends and found out the following information:

Favourite Ice Cream Flavour Survey

Chocolate 15   Piña Colada 2
Strawberry 3   Rocky Road 12
Bubble Gum 7   Chocolate Chip 8
Vanilla 10   Others 4

a. Construct a pictograph to display this information.

b. Construct a bar graph to display this information.

c. Describe any differences between the two graphs. Does one give a clearer display? Why or why not?

2. Jana wants to ride her bicycle on a 27-km route when she goes on vacation. To get ready, she rides every day and keeps track of her kilometres. Make a line plot using her data.

6 km, 9 km, 8 km, 11 km, 10 km, 13 km, 14 km, 14 km, 12 km, 15 km, 14 km, 16 km, 16 km, 15 km, 15 km, 16 km, 17 km, 18 km, 16 km, 17 km, 17 km, 18 km, 17 km, 19 km, 17 km, 18 km, 18 km, 20 km, 18 km, 19 km, 20 km, 22 km, 21 km, 24 km, 23 km, 24 km, 25 km, 25 km, 26 km, 25 km, 26 km

a. What is the number that occurs most often (mode) in your line plot?

b. What is the middle-most (median) number of kilometres?

c. How many kilometres long do you think Jana's typical ride was when she trained? Explain your thinking.

d. Explain whether you think Jana will be able to complete the 27-km ride.

3. Choose an event in which you are interested that requires training. Make a line plot that could be used as a training plan. Set this as a goal and write how you would act on your plan.

1. Mimi collected these data about how long it takes her classmates to get to school.

Travel Time to School	Number of Students
0 to 5 min	||
6 to 10 min	☰ |||
11 to 15 min	☰ ☰ ||
16 to 20 min	||||
more than 20 min		

   a. What is the typical travel time to get to school?
   b. How many students' travel times are reflected in these data?
   c. Make a graph of these data.

2. The table shows the days it rains at a holiday resort, on average.

   a. If you wanted to avoid rain, when would you take your holiday?
   b. Explain how these data might have been collected.

Month	Number of Days of Rain
January	10
February	8
March	4
April	3
May	1
June	2
July	1
August	1
September	2
October	3
November	5
December	8

3. Choose something you would like to know about your classmates.
   a. What question would you ask?
   b. How would you collect and organize the data?
   c. How would you display the data?

4. Write three statements about this graph.

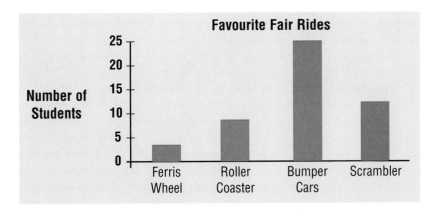

5. What might the following graph represent?
Make up labels for a, b, c, and d.
What scale could be used up the side?
Give the graph a title.

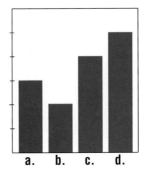

6. Imagine a bar graph for each of the following.
How would you label each axis?
   a. the number of people who like to play each of three different sports
   b. what pets your classmates have
   c. the colours of cars in a parking lot

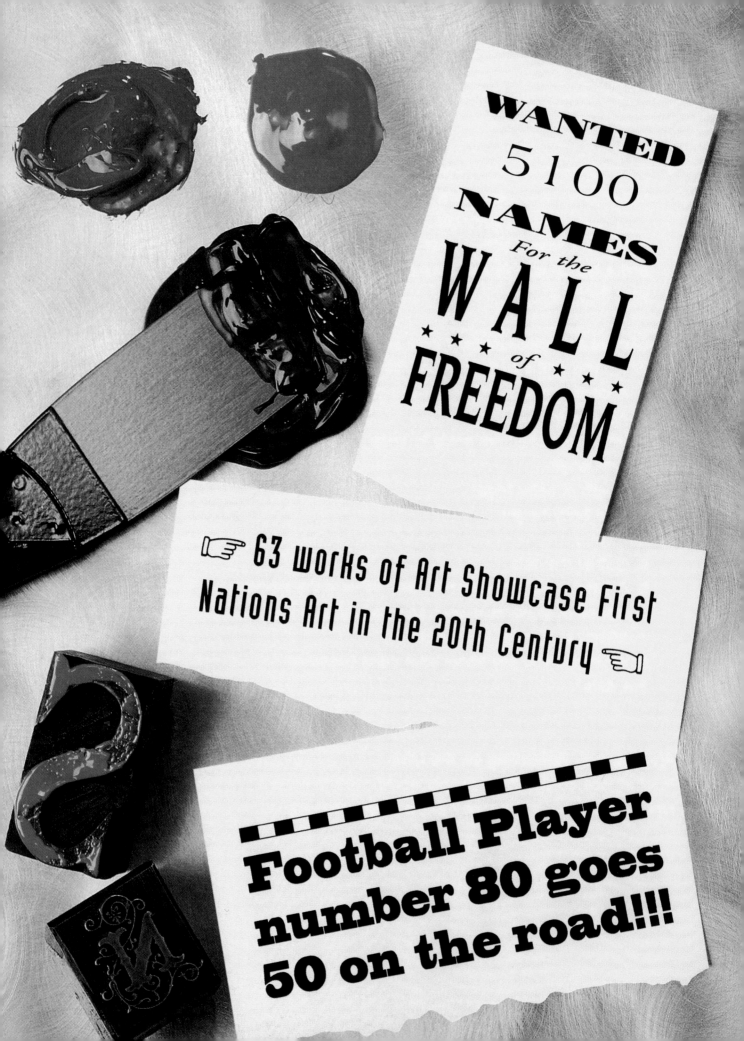

GRAND DISPLAY of 1200 Lilac Trees in HAMILTON

*H*ow can we show numbers?

TOONTOWN visitors enjoy 10 000 LAUGHS!

REPRESENTING NUMBERS

STARTING OUT

★10 000 POINTS★ WIN★A★FREE★GAME!

1 • Which player is closest to a free game?
How do you know?

• Who needs the most points for a free game?
Explain your thinking.

• About how many more points would the player with
the highest number of points need to get a free game?

My Journal: Which game would you
like to be playing? Why?

REPRESENTING NUMBERS

S·T·A·R·T·I·N·G OUT

World Record

Arrow shot
1872 m

World Record

Bed pushed
5204 km

World Record

Fastest English Channel swim
7 hours 30 minutes

World Record

Riding a sea wave
1.8 km

World Record

Brick carried
99.4 km

World Record

Egg and spoon race
3 hours 47 minutes over 42 km

World Record

Kite flown
180 hours 17 minutes

World Record

Scout knots tied
6 in 8.1 seconds

World Record

Longest swim
2938 km

World Record

Leap frogging
1603 km
in 244 hours 43 minutes

World Record

Running backward
4 hours 15 seconds
over 43.5 km

2
- Which record is about ten times as far as another record?

- Which record took about ten times as long as another record?

- Which two records took place over about the same distance?

- How could you order the data you see here? Write your answer and explain why you did it that way.

- Is there a way to compare all the data? Explain your thinking.

World Record

Balancing milk bottle
104 km in 20 hours 43 minutes

World Record

Longest canoe journey
19 603 km

My Journal: Write about something that would take you more than 1000 seconds to do. Explain how you arrived at your answer.

Estimating and Counting Objects

▶ How can you find out about how many beads are in the jar?

How many in a handful?

1

How many cover 25 squares?

2

How many in 10 g?

3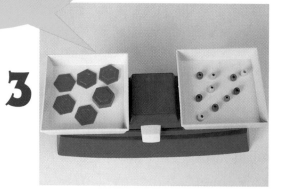

How many in a scoop?

4

ON YOUR OWN

1. Each grid has 100 small squares. Estimate the number of squares shaded for each.

a. b.

c. d.

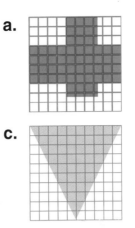

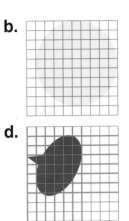

2. There are 20 sheets of paper in the small pile. Estimate the number of sheets in the larger pile.

3. This book has about 400 pages. Between which pages do you think the bookmark is placed? Explain your thinking.

4. *My Journal:* When might you estimate rather than count?

Practise Your Skills

1. 345, 293, 534, 750, 545, 554, 378
   Which number above is closest to each number below?
   a. 300   **b.** 400   **c.** 500   **d.** 600

2. Round each number to the nearest 10.
   a. 74   **b.** 629   **c.** 843   **d.** 709

3. Which do you estimate to be closest to your age?
   a. 500 months   **b.** 500 weeks   **c.** 500 hours

Visualizing Numbers

Estimate the number shown by each group of blocks. Then count to find the number. Write the number as a numeral and in words; then read the number.

1.

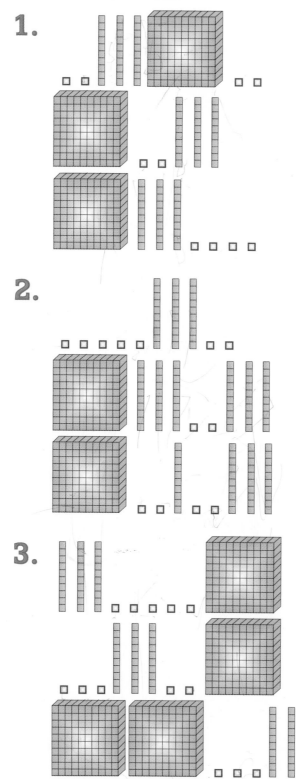

2.

3.

1. Write four numbers between 250 and 850. Draw base ten blocks to show each. Then write your numbers in words.

2. Write a number that is less than 700, greater than 600, and has 0 tens. Draw base ten blocks to show your number. Then write your number in words.

3. How many multiples of 10 are there from 245 to 375? Remember, multiples of 10 end in 0.

4. How many times would the digit 5 be printed in writing the numbers 1 to 250? Prove your answer.

5. *My Journal:* What questions do you have about reading and writing numbers?

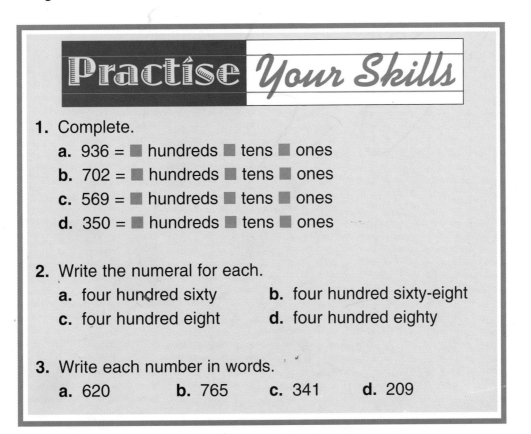

Practise Your Skills

1. Complete.
   a. 936 = ■ hundreds ■ tens ■ ones
   b. 702 = ■ hundreds ■ tens ■ ones
   c. 569 = ■ hundreds ■ tens ■ ones
   d. 350 = ■ hundreds ■ tens ■ ones

2. Write the numeral for each.
   a. four hundred sixty
   b. four hundred sixty-eight
   c. four hundred eight
   d. four hundred eighty

3. Write each number in words.
   a. 620
   b. 765
   c. 341
   d. 209

Representing Large Numbers

▶ How can you use blocks to build 1000?

Build numbers using the blocks listed. Read each number.
Write each number as a numeral and in words.

- 1 thousand, 3 hundreds, 6 tens, 7 ones

- 2 thousands, 5 tens, 5 ones

- 1 thousand, 8 hundreds

- 3 thousands, 2 hundreds, 9 ones

ON YOUR OWN

1. Find examples of headlines or articles in the newspaper that show large numbers. Bring them to class to share.
   a. Read the numbers aloud.
   b. Write the numbers in words.

2. *My Journal:* What do you find difficult working with large numbers? What do you find easy? Explain.

Practise Your Skills

1. Complete.
   a. 9306 = ■ thousands ■ hundreds ■ tens ■ ones
   b. 7352 = ■ thousands ■ hundreds ■ tens ■ ones
   c. 5069 = ■ thousands ■ hundreds ■ tens ■ ones
   d. 3500 = ■ thousands ■ hundreds ■ tens ■ ones

2. Write the numeral for each.
   a. four thousand three hundred sixty
   b. seven thousand four hundred seventy-one
   c. four thousand six hundred eight
   d. three thousand sixty-five

3. Write each number in words.
   a. 6200   b. 1765   c. 3041   d. 8209

Representing Numbers in Many Ways

▶ In how many ways can you show 142, using hundreds, tens, and ones?

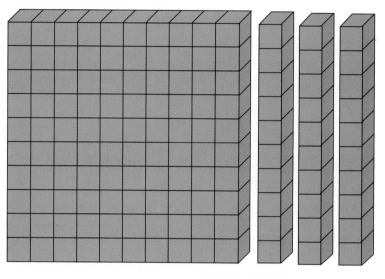

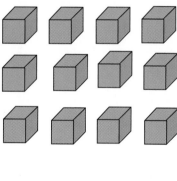

Hundreds	Tens	Ones
1	4	2
1	3	12

▶ Find as many ways as you can to show 1420 using thousands, hundreds, and tens.

Thousands	Hundreds	Tens	Ones
1	4	2	0
0	14	2	0

ON YOUR OWN

1. How many different ways can you show 53¢ using dimes and pennies?

2. How many different ways can you show $1.25 using loonies, dimes, and pennies?

3. Mr. Rasheed is going to buy a horse for $2000. How many bills would he give if he paid for the horse in $100 bills? in $10 bills? Explain how you arrived at your answers.

4. *My Journal:* How can you show numbers in different ways?

Practise Your Skills

1. Write each number using numerals and words.

   a.   b.

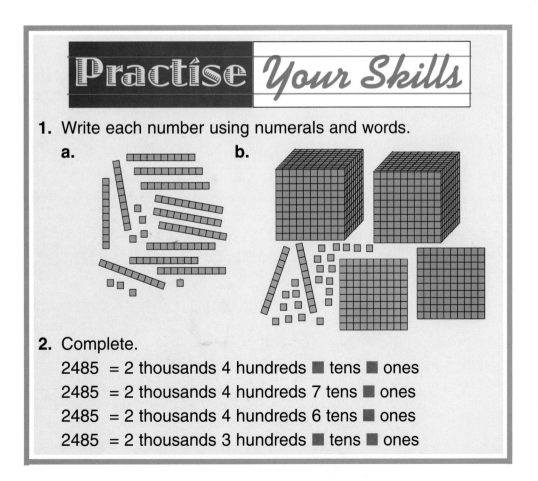

2. Complete.

   2485 = 2 thousands 4 hundreds ■ tens ■ ones
   2485 = 2 thousands 4 hundreds 7 tens ■ ones
   2485 = 2 thousands 4 hundreds 6 tens ■ ones
   2485 = 2 thousands 3 hundreds ■ tens ■ ones

Group
· ·

2 players

Materials
· ·

Each player needs:
- a set of ten cards labelled 0, 1, 2, 3, 4, 5, 6, 7, 8, 9
- a set of five place value cards labelled ones, tens, hundreds, thousands, ten thousands

Game Rules:
· ·

1 Each player arranges his/her place value cards in order in one row. Start with ten thousands on the left and end with ones on the right.

2 Shuffle the two decks of number cards. Turn them face down.

3 Each player draws a card; the greater number goes first.

4 The first player turns over one number card and places it above any of her/his place value cards.

5 The second player turns over one number card and places it above any of his/her place value cards.

6 The game continues until each player has filled five place value positions with numbers.

7 Players compare the two numbers to find the greater number.

8 The player with the greater number wins!

DIAL 6284 FOR MATH

Have you ever wondered about ways other people used to represent numbers? Around 450 B.C.E., the people of Alexandria in northern Africa used a system of letters to represent numbers. The chart shows what some of the letters represented.

People today use letters for numbers. To make telephone numbers easier to remember, many businesses choose four- or seven-digit numbers that spell out appropriate words. A weather network, for example, may use a telephone number that contains the word WIND.

A	represented	1
B	represented	2
E	represented	5
F	represented	6
H	represented	8
I	represented	10
K	represented	20
M	represented	40
N	represented	50
O	represented	70
P	represented	100
T	represented	300
X	represented	600

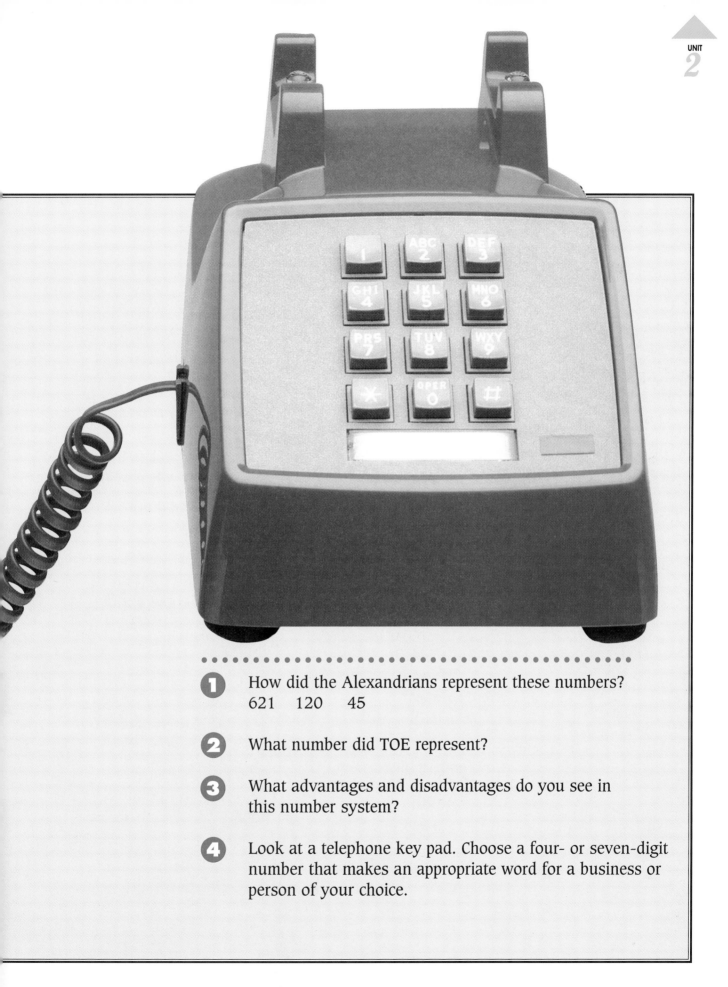

1 How did the Alexandrians represent these numbers?
621   120   45

2 What number did TOE represent?

3 What advantages and disadvantages do you see in this number system?

4 Look at a telephone key pad. Choose a four- or seven-digit number that makes an appropriate word for a business or person of your choice.

Comparing and Ordering Numbers

▶ Which shows are most popular with children? with teenagers? Which shows are the most popular overall?

Music of the Week
The top 10 CDs for the week are reviewed. Music groups often perform (half hour)

Au Revoir!
A comedy about the daily activities of a French family (half hour)

Plumber's Helper
A show specializing in helpful hints about fixing broken plumbing fixtures (half hour)

Order in the Court
Interesting courtroom stories told from the plaintiff's and defendant's points of view (1 hour)

Mysteries, Mysteries, Mysteries
A drama taking place in different locations showing detectives solving crimes (1 hour)

The Warthogs
An animated show about a family of six (half hour)

Sea Diver
An hour-long adventure story starring two divers who specialize in locating and recovering lost treasures (1 hour)

What's New in Electronics?

An introduction of the newest electronic products available
(half hour)

Room 14

A show about the funny and serious events occurring in a grade 4 classroom
(1 hour)

40/40

An in-depth analysis of four issues currently in the news
(1 hour)

Top Ten Television Shows in Green City					
	Audience				
Show	under 12	13-18	19-35	36-55	56+
Music of the Week	8 467	6 804	5 197	2 225	890
Au Revoir!	4 685	512	243	432	776
Plumber's Helper	109	413	8106	24 725	7 996
Order in the Court	786	632	8 431	5 842	2 948
Sea Diver	4 634	8 973	9 542	10 906	6 542
40/40	531	2 786	8 506	15 040	4 542
What's New in Electronics?	8 957	16 947	17 046	13 486	4 807
Room 14	5 731	3 543	507	352	165
Mysteries	708	1 841	14 354	17 735	9 784
The Warthogs	26 009	17 846	8 957	6 534	863

ON YOUR OWN

1. **a.** Do you think these populations are exact numbers or estimates? Explain your thinking.

Populations	
Cayman Islands	26 000
Monaco	38 500
Virgin Islands	12 900
American Samoa	43 000
Falkland Islands	2 000
Saint Kitts-Nevis	40 000
Liechtenstein	28 400

   b. Which places listed have populations less than the population of the Cayman Islands?

   c. Which place listed has the greatest population?

   d. List the places in order from least to greatest population.

   e. San Marino has a population of about 23 000. Where would it fit on your list?

   f. Which three places have a combined population of about 41 000?

2. Use the data in the table below.

Air Distance in Kilometres						
	Calgary	Halifax	Montreal	Saskatoon	Toronto	Vancouver
Calgary		3742	3003	323	2686	686
Halifax	3742		805	2067	1286	4424
Montreal	3003	805		1560	509	3679
Saskatoon	323	2067	1560		1379	750
Toronto	2686	1286	509	1379		3343
Vancouver	686	4424	3679	750	3343	

a. What is the distance between Montreal and Vancouver?

b. What is the least distance in the table?

c. Which two cities listed are farthest apart?

d. Which city is farthest from Saskatoon?

e. Imagine that the cities were located on a straight line.
   Draw a line and mark the position of each city.

●——●

Vancouver   Halifax

3. *My Journal:* What strategies do you use to compare large
   numbers?

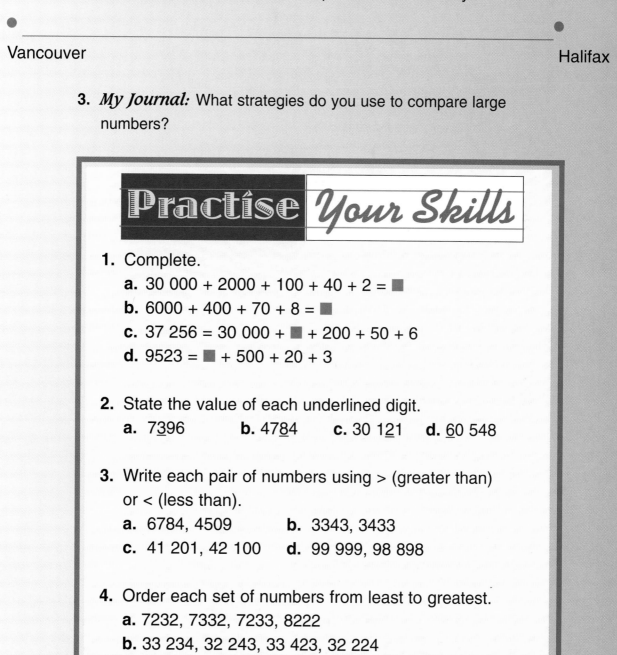

Practise Your Skills

1. Complete.
   a. 30 000 + 2000 + 100 + 40 + 2 = ■
   b. 6000 + 400 + 70 + 8 = ■
   c. 37 256 = 30 000 + ■ + 200 + 50 + 6
   d. 9523 = ■ + 500 + 20 + 3

2. State the value of each underlined digit.
   a. 7396   b. 4784   c. 30 121   d. 60 548

3. Write each pair of numbers using > (greater than)
   or < (less than).
   a. 6784, 4509   b. 3343, 3433
   c. 41 201, 42 100   d. 99 999, 98 898

4. Order each set of numbers from least to greatest.
   a. 7232, 7332, 7233, 8222
   b. 33 234, 32 243, 33 423, 32 224

DESIGN A BASE TEN KIT

Price List

Unit cubes	$0.03 each
Tens rods	$0.30 each
Hundreds flats	$1.00 each
Thousands cubes	$7.00 each

Your job
is to design
the "ideal" kit of
base ten blocks.

- Make sure your kit
  contains enough blocks
  for a class of 30 students
  to model numbers to 10 000.

- Decide whether or not to include
  a 10 000 block. Draw to show what a
  10 000 block would look like.

- Calculate the cost of the kit.

- Write a memo to the president of the company
  with your recommendations and your reasoning.

Check YOURSELF

Great job! Your base ten kit shows a clear understanding
of place value concepts. You communicated your ideas
well and showed clear thinking.

1. Draw a chart like this. Which blocks will you need to make 400? Draw base ten blocks to show your answers. Then write the number you need to make 400.

You Start With:	Blocks You Need:	Number You Need:
362		
99		
242		
38		

2. Think of a number that fits each set of clues. Write your number and then draw base ten blocks to show it.

   a. The number is less than 500 and greater than 400. It has 1 ten.

   b. The number is between 750 and 850. It has 0 tens.

   c. The number is between 283 and 299. It is a multiple of ten.

   d. The number is between 600 and 700. The digits are all even. The sum of the digits is 12.

3. There are 100 pegs on this geoboard. How many geoboards like it would it take to have 1000 pegs? 10 000 pegs? Explain your thinking.

4. Write the missing number from each cheque.

   a.

   J. SMITH THEYERA
   99 ALIVANI ST.
   TORONTO, ONTARIO   0035 - A
                                              19
   PAY TO THE
   ORDER OF $ 1750.00
                                    /100DOLLARS
   B COMMERCIAL DEPOSITS E.
   B🄴E 2921 B LAKESHORE ST NORTH
          TORONTO, ONTARIO
   MEMO
   5235 ⋆ 523523⋆523⋆523⋆523523

   b.

   J. SMITH THEYERA
   99 ALIVANI ST.
   TORONTO, ONTARIO   0035 - A
                                              19
   PAY TO THE
   ORDER OF $
   twelve thousand eighty-five   00/100DOLLARS
   B COMMERCIAL DEPOSITS E.
   B🄴E 2921 B LAKESHORE ST NORTH
          TORONTO, ONTARIO
   MEMO
   5235 ⋆ 523523⋆523⋆523⋆523523

5. Draw base ten blocks for each set of clues.
   a. These blocks show 379.
   b. There are 17 blocks. These blocks show 53.
   c. There are 24 blocks. These blocks show 168.
   d. Write a set of clues for blocks for someone else to solve.

6. Write another name for each number.
   a. 15 tens
   b. 15 hundreds
   c. 15 thousands

7. Use each set of digits to make:
   a. the greatest possible number
   b. the least possible number

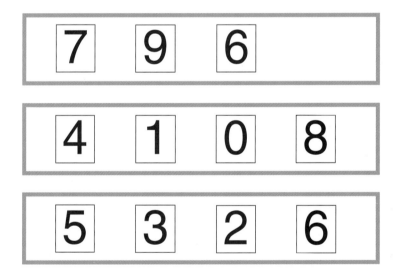

8. Find six 5-digit numbers in a newspaper and record them.
   Order them from least to greatest.

9. Look through some newspapers or magazines to find ten
   numbers you think will add up to 10 000. Add them.
   How close to 10 000 were you?

S K I L L
BANK
FROM THIS UNIT

1. Which number is closest to 560?

650,   605,   556,   565,   506

2. Write the numeral for each.
   a. four thousand two hundred eighteen
   b. six hundred eighty
   c. two thousand fifty-six
   d. ten thousand seven hundred ninety

3. Write each number in words.
   a. 9465   **b.** 4063   **c.** 75 407   **d.** 11 346

4. Name the numbers.
   a.   **b.**

5. Which numbers represent 6840?
   a. six thousand eight hundred forty
   b. 6000 + 80 + 40   **c.** 6000 + 700 + 140
   d. 6 thousands 8 hundreds 3 tens 10 ones
   e. sixty thousand eight hundred forty
   f. 6 thousands 8 hundreds 4 tens

6. Which is greater:
   a. 784 or 748?   **b.** 4330 or 3430?
   c. 9789 or 9879?   **d.** 23 670 or 32 760?

SKILL BANK

LOOKING BACK

1. This table shows distances travelled by students on holidays.

Student	Distance Travelled
Rosalia	1000 km
Sheree	280 km
Daniel	50 km
Mica	200 km
Connor	500 km
Eric	250 km
Hillary	300 km

a. Who travelled the farthest?

b. Who travelled farther than Sheree?

c. What was the mean distance travelled?

d. Do you think distances are exact or estimates? Explain.

e. Make a graph to display these data.

2. This graph shows the results of a survey of students' favourite computer uses.

Favourite Computer Uses of Students

(Bar graph — Computer Uses vs Number of Students)
- Internet: about 3
- Encyclopedia: about 4
- Drawing: about 8
- Writing: about 8
- Games: 20

a. What is the most popular use? least popular?

b. How many students were in the survey?

c. How do you think the results of a survey of the students in your class would compare to these data?

UNIT

3

Analyzing Triangles and Quadrilaterals

*H*ow can we describe figures?

**ANALYZING TRIANGLES
AND QUADRILATERALS**

S·T·A·R·T·I·N·G
OUT

1 • What figures can you see in these constellations?

• How many different figures could you make out of each constellation?

• How are the figures in these constellations alike? How are they different?

• Use dot paper to create your own constellation. Or, trace a set of dots from one of these constellation maps. Name your constellation. Describe it using figures.

My Journal: What do you know about figures?

**ANALYZING TRIANGLES
AND QUADRILATERALS**

S·T·A·R·T·I·N·G
OUT

2 Use this picture for a
figure scavenger hunt.
Your challenge is
to find at least:

- 2 parallelograms
- 2 trapezoids
- 15 triangles
- 8 squares
- 2 rectangles
  that are the
  same size

3 What other figures can
you find?

- Which figures in this
  picture do you see
  in your classroom?
  Describe what you see.

- Create a scavenger
  hunt list for a friend.
  Use figures in the
  classroom.

My Journal: What figures do
you see most often around you?
Why do you think this is so?

Words to Know

A **triangle** is a three-sided figure.

A **parallelogram** is a four-sided figure. Its opposite sides are parallel and the same length.

A **rectangle** is a four-sided figure. It has four right angles.

A **square** is a four-sided figure. It has four right angles. It has four sides the same length.

A **trapezoid** is a four-sided figure. It has only one pair of parallel sides.

Exploring Triangles

▶ Use these guidelines to try to make a triangle with three pieces of string.

1 Take a length of string.

2 Decide where to make the two cuts.

3 Cut the string into three pieces.

4 Try to make a triangle with the pieces. Make sure the pieces are as straight as possible. Make sure the ends touch.

5 Measure the length of each piece to the nearest centimetre. Record the lengths in a chart.

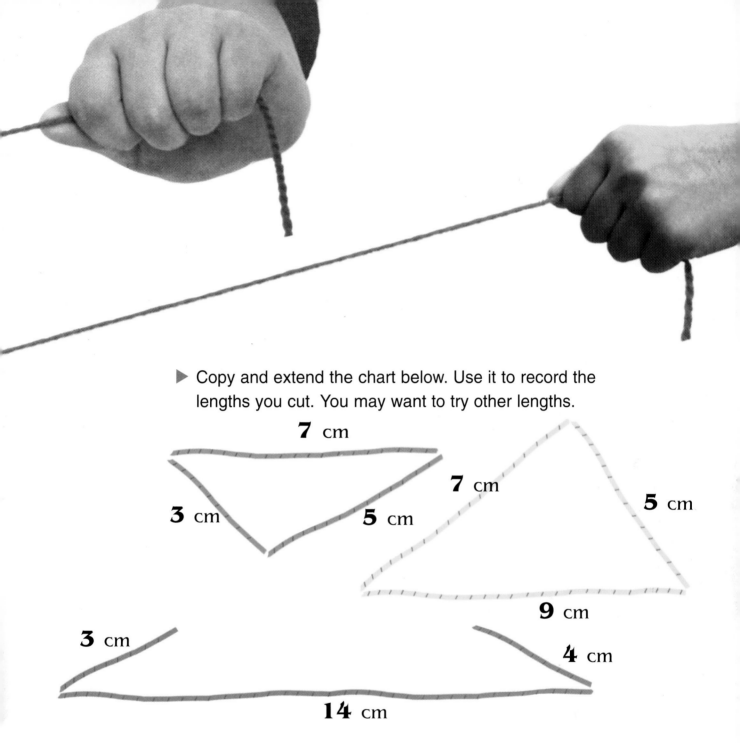

▶ Copy and extend the chart below. Use it to record the lengths you cut. You may want to try other lengths.

Lengths of Pieces	Length of Longest Side	Length of Other two Sides	Triangle?
7 cm, 3 cm, 5 cm	7 cm	3 cm, 5 cm	yes
3 cm, 14 cm, 4 cm	14 cm	3 cm, 4 cm	no
7 cm, 5 cm, 9 cm	9 cm	7 cm, 5 cm	yes

Soaring SYMMETRY

Have you ever wondered why so many things that fly through the air are shaped like triangles? As far back as 4000 years ago, hunters used flint arrowheads in the shape of isosceles triangles. Even arrows you see today on an archery range have heads shaped that way.

An isosceles triangle is a good shape for things that fly, such as arrowheads, paper airplanes, and darts. An isosceles triangle has line symmetry. Two of its sides are identical, which makes it fly straight.

You can make an isosceles triangle. Fold a piece of paper in half. Then cut along the diagonal line.

The two sides you created with one cut
are the same length. The two angles
at the bottom corners are the same size.
Both halves of the triangle are identical –
it's line symmetry at work!

1 Now make an isosceles triangle
that flies – a paper airplane!
Remember the symmetry.
Everything you do to one side
of the plane, you have to do to
the other side.

1. Fold paper
in half
lengthwise.
Open it to
create a
centre
line.

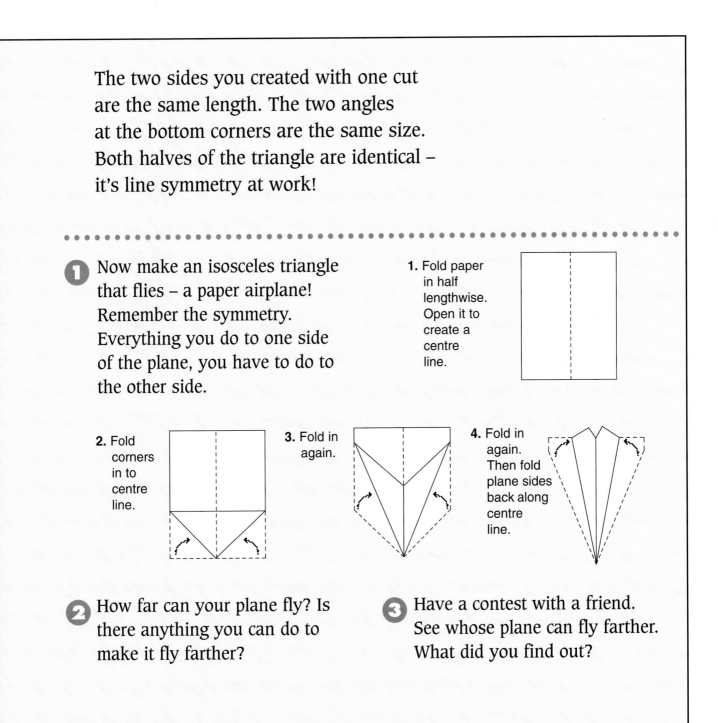

2. Fold
corners
in to
centre
line.

3. Fold in
again.

4. Fold in
again.
Then fold
plane sides
back along
centre
line.

2 How far can your plane fly? Is
there anything you can do to
make it fly farther?

3 Have a contest with a friend.
See whose plane can fly farther.
What did you find out?

Sides of Triangles

All sides of a triangle can
be different lengths.
Scalene means "uneven" or "odd."
It comes from a word meaning
serpent.

All sides of a triangle
can be the same length.
Equilateral means "equal sides."

Two sides of a triangle
can be the same length.
Isosceles means "equal legs."

ON
YOUR
OWN

1. Look for triangles at home and in your neighbourhood. What kinds do you find? What are the different
kinds of triangles used for? Copy and complete the
chart to record your
findings. Then write
about what you found.

2. *My Journal:* What
have you learned about
triangles so far?

Type of Triangle	Use

Angles in Triangles

Angles in Triangles

▶ How can you classify the triangles in these stained-glass windows?

ON YOUR OWN

1. How could you group these letters by their angles?

A, E, F, H, I, K, L, M, N, T, V, W, X, Y, Z

2. What is the greatest number of right angles a triangle can have?
What is the greatest number of angles greater than a right angle
a triangle can have?
What is the greatest number of angles less than a right angle
a triangle can have?
Write or draw to show your thinking.

3. Is it possible to have a triangle with one of each of the three kinds
of angles? Draw pictures to help show your answer.

4. *My Journal:* What did you learn that was new?

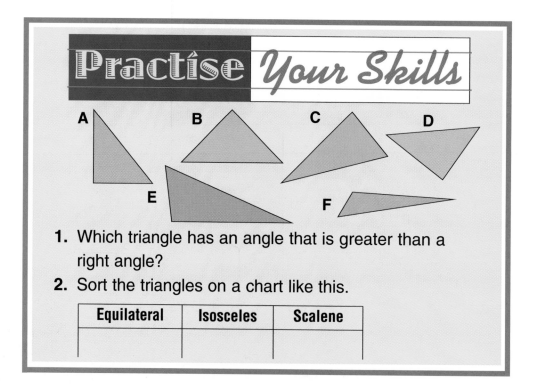

Practise Your Skills

1. Which triangle has an angle that is greater than a
right angle?

2. Sort the triangles on a chart like this.

Equilateral	Isosceles	Scalene

Types of Quadrilaterals

▶ Use your Power Polygons to make these quadrilaterals.
Describe each figure. Include these figures on your chart.

Figures within Figures

ON YOUR OWN

Look at the quilt below.

1. How can you use parallelograms to make a bigger parallelogram?

2. Which is the largest parallelogram you can find in this design?

3. How many small parallelograms would you estimate there are in all?

4. What patterns do you see that can help you find all the parallelograms of different sizes?

5. *My Journal:* What did you find interesting about finding squares and parallelograms? Explain.

FIND THE
FIGURES

Pick one figure from the Power Polygons. Design a "hidden figure" puzzle of your own. Tell the puzzle solver what kind of figure to look for.

CheckYOURSELF

Great job! Your puzzle included a variety of hidden figures in different sizes and/or positions. The puzzle was interesting for another student to solve – but not too difficult! Your explanation of the answer was clear and complete.

P R O B L E M
BANK

1. Make a list of words that begin with "tri," for instance, Triceratops, triple, and so on. What do they all have in common?

2.

Trace all the triangles you can see in the picture.

3. In the chart below, the lengths of 2 sides of a triangle are given. Copy the chart. Fill in a length for the third side so that a triangle can be formed.

Longest Side	Other 2 Sides
9 cm	4 cm, ■ cm
■ cm	6 cm, 3 cm
7 cm	2 cm, ■ cm
5 cm	■ cm, 4 cm
■ cm	6 cm, 8 cm
15 cm	2 cm, ■ cm

4. Create a pattern for a stained-glass window. Use different types of triangles. Describe the pattern you created. What types of triangles did you use?

5.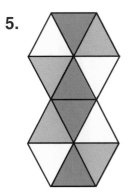

    a. How many triangles are in this design?

    b. What kind of triangles are they?

    c. Use Power Polygons or a drawing. Try to make a design with 20 triangles that are all the same kind.

6. Compare these 3 triangles. Make a chart showing how they are alike and how they are different.

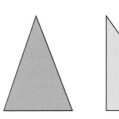 

7. Draw a square. Draw a rectangle that is not a square. Divide each figure into triangles by joining two vertices. What kinds of triangles did you make? Why do you think that is so?

8. Matching triangles can be combined to create a quadrilateral. Draw and cut out two matching triangles. Tape them together to form a quadrilateral. Repeat using different triangles. Record your findings in a chart. Draw the triangles you used. Draw the quadrilaterals that you made.

9. Do you think it will be easy to design a floor pattern using figures that have at least one right angle in each piece? Explain your thinking. Try it with Power Polygons or paper cutouts.

1. Why is an equilateral triangle sometimes called an equiangular triangle?

2. Draw any three triangles. Write equilateral, scalene, or isosceles for each triangle.

3. **a.** Which figure below is not a quadrilateral?

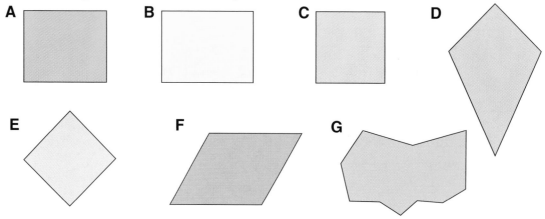

A B C D

E F G

b. Sort the quadrilaterals on a chart like this.

All Sides Equal	Two Pairs of Equal Sides	No Sides Equal	Four Right Angles	One Pair of Parallel Sides	Two Pairs of Parallel Sides

4. Draw a figure that is in some way the same as each figure shown. Describe how each pair of figures is the same.

a. b.

SKILL BANK
LOOKING BACK

1. Use the graph.
   a. Which two activities are equally popular?
   b. How many students like reading best? like movies best?
   c. How many more students like watching movies better than reading?
   d. How many more students like to do the most popular activity than to do the least popular activity?

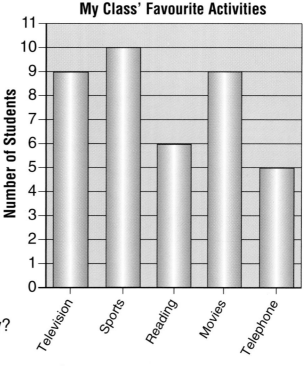

My Class' Favourite Activities

Number of Students (0–11)

Television, Sports, Reading, Movies, Telephone

2. Which number is closest to 79 879?
   79 989   79 889   99 879   69 879

3. Round each number to the nearest 100.
   a. 238   **b.** 487   **c.** 2540   **d.** 13 764

4. Write each group of numbers in order from least to greatest.
   a. 345, 436, 354, 435
   b. 9053, 9578, 8935, 9875
   c. 12 510, 37 510, 21 150, 12 015

What operations can we use?

For my party, we need:
11 ~~to~~ hats
10 loot bags + 1 for me
20 hot dogs + 3 for me

1 <u>Big</u> Cake

10 Candles
2 Cartons of ice cream
4 game prizes
5 litres of juice

PARTY SUPPLIES

OPEN EVERY DAY FOR YOUR BIRTHDAY

11 HATS @ $0.50 EACH $ 0.50
1 PKG OF 12 PAPER PLATES $ 2.70
25 BALLOONS @ $0.09 EACH $ 2.25
1 PKG of 20 FORKS $ 1.49
1 PKG NAPKINS $ 2.99

SUBTOTAL $14.98
7% PST $ 1.05
7% GST $ 1.05
TOTAL $17.08

EVERYTHING YOU WANT IN A PARTY STORE!

1 • The four basic math operations are addition, subtraction, multiplication, and division. What operations are suggested in the picture?

• What might each person be thinking about her or his purchases?

• Write some problems based on the picture. Make sure that operations are needed to solve them.

My Journal: How can operations help you when you are shopping?

S·T·A·R·T·I·N·G OUT

Sammy's Food Mart

Pink grapefruit
3 for $0.99

Sliced roast beef
$8.50/kg

Black Forest Ham
$1.10/100g

Navel oranges
4/$1.99

corn flakes
$1.29 400g Box

Rice Crisps cereal
$2.88 475g Box

chicken soup
2/$0.97

vegetable soup
2/$0.88

chicken
$4.17/kg

Bathroom tissue
12 pkg
$3.88
12 roll pkg

Bread $0.99

Pannini Rolls
6 for $1.49

milk $1.29/L

milk
milk $3.29/4L

Shopping List

6 grapefruit
2 L milk
kg roast beef
cans soup
box corn
flakes
read

2 • Estimate the total cost of the groceries on the list.

• About how much change would there be from $20.00?

• About how much would one grapefruit cost?

• About how much would a dozen oranges cost?

• Which is a better buy, roast beef or ham?

• Write some problems using any of the information from the flyer. Make sure that you have at least one problem for each of the four operations.

My Journal: Write a definition for each of the four operations.

Adding and Subtracting

▶ How many days have you spent in school in your life?

Here's some information to get you started:

1 year = 365 days
1 year =   12 months
1 year =   52 weeks

Words to Know

sum: the number you obtain by adding numbers
12 + 13 = (25 ← sum)

difference: the number you obtain by subtracting one number from another
25 – 12 = (13 ← difference)

ON YOUR OWN

1. Estimate each sum or difference.
   Then add or subtract using any procedures
   you like. Show all your work.
   a. 354 + 879   **b.** 8642 − 403
   c. $22.85 + $65.23 **d.** $865.00 − $427.00
   e. 2071 + 7069   **f.** 9980 − 1460

2. Find two numbers whose sum is 946. Now find
   three other pairs of numbers whose sum is 946.

3. Find two numbers whose difference is 585. Now find three
   other pairs of numbers whose difference is 585.

4. For each expression, write a story problem that could
   be solved by doing that calculation. Then solve the
   problem showing all your work.
   a. $527 + $860   **b.** 8538 − 4293

5. *My Journal:* How do you check your work for addition?
   for subtraction?

Practise Your Skills

Find the sums.

1. 300	**2.** 607	**3.** 552	**4.** 876	**5.** 458
+900	+ 314	+ 436	+ 519	+ 293

Find the differences.

6. 650	**7.** 650	**8.** 791	**9.** 932	**10.** 1286
−130	− 190	− 287	− 188	− 736

Strategies for Addition and Subtraction

▶ How did each student find 7695 + 2086?

▶ How did each student find 9842 − 6328?

Chalkboard Talk

$$
\begin{array}{r}
7695 \\
+\,2086 \\
\hline
9000 \\
+\quad 700 \\
+\qquad 81 \\
\hline
9781
\end{array}
$$

$$
\begin{array}{r}
9842 \\
-\,6328 \\
\hline
3000 \\
+\quad 500 \\
+\qquad 14 \\
\hline
3514
\end{array}
$$

7695   add 5 → 7700
+ 2086   take away 5 → +2081

9842   add 2 → 9844
− 6328   to each → −6330
  3514

1. These students added 379 and 534.

"First I add the ones, and trade 10 ones for a ten. Then I add the tens and trade 10 tens for a hundred. Then I add the hundreds."

"First I add 379 and 500. That's 879. Then I count on 3 tens, 889, 899, 909 and add 4 ones, 910, 911, 912, 913."

How does your method of adding compare?
Draw a picture of yourself with a thought bubble that tells how you would add 697 and 842.

2. Fiona signed 538 letters on the weekend and 916 during the week. How many did she sign altogether?

3. Jacob delivered 465 flyers. He has 535 more to deliver. How many flyers did he start with?

4. Write a story problem with two or three numbers with a sum of more than 1000. Explain how you would solve the problem.

ON
YOUR
OWN

5. These students subtracted 486 from 935.

"I need more ones so I can trade a ten for 10 ones, then subtract the ones. I need more tens. I trade a hundred for 10 tens and subtract the tens. Then I subtract the hundreds."

"If I add 14 to 486 I get 500. So I subtract 500 from 935 to get 435, then add 14. The answer is 449."

$$935 - 486$$

$$\overset{2\ 15}{9\cancel{3}5} - 486 \atop 9$$

$$\overset{8\ 12\ 15}{\cancel{9}\cancel{3}5} - 486 \atop 49$$

$$\overset{8\ 12\ 15}{\cancel{9}\cancel{3}5} - 486 \atop 449$$

How does your method of subtracting compare? Draw a picture of yourself with a thought bubble that tells how you would solve 836 – 598.

6. Katie has 500 invitations to send. She has sent 388. How many more does she have to send?

7. Ryan delivered 8786 posters. Sheree delivered 6394. Who delivered more posters? how many more?

8. Write a story problem that can be solved using subtraction. Explain how you would solve the problem.

9. You have a $10.00 bill. You want to buy a pair of socks for $2.49, a belt for $4.98, and a baseball cap for $1.95. How will you find out if you have enough money? Should you estimate, use mental math, or use a calculator? Explain your choice.

10. Jessica's family was driving to Halifax, a distance of about 780 km. They drove 490 km the first day. How much farther did they have to go?

11. Jonah's family flew 509 km from Montreal to Toronto and 3343 km from Toronto to Vancouver. What is the total distance they flew?

12. Anh spent $12.98 and $36.77. She started out with $65.00. How much does she have left?

13. *My Journal:* How do you decide which strategies and procedures to use to add and subtract large numbers?

Practise Your Skills

Add or subtract.

| 1. | 369 + 29 | 2. 504 + 296 | 3. 1376 + 416 | 4. 1161 + 6432 | 5. 1545 + 5822 |

| 6. | 662 − 450 | 7. 937 − 624 | 8. 806 − 212 | 9. 9267 − 209 | 10. 4218 − 1976 |

11. 447 + 239   12. 374 + 996   13. 2404 + 335   14. 2388 + 3840

15. 663 − 555   16. 608 − 293   17. 2467 − 365   18. 3840 − 2388

The Quick Addition Game

Group
· ·

2 players

Materials
· ·

Each player needs:

• Recording sheet

• Calculator

• Paper and pencil

Game Rules

1. Decide who will be Player A and who will be Player B.

2. Player A records an addition example with two four-digit numbers on the recording sheet.

3. Player B quickly estimates the sum and Player A records it.

4. Both players use paper and pencil to find the exact answer. Player A records it.

5. Both players use paper and pencil to find the difference between the exact answer and the estimate. The difference is recorded as Player B's score.

6. Any disagreements in sums or differences can be settled with a calculator.

7. Play continues for five rounds. Then the players switch roles and play again.

8. Both players calculate their total scores. The player with the lowest total wins.

The Quick Addition Game		Player _____	
Question	Estimate	Exact Answer	Score
1.			
2.			
3.			
4.			
5.			
		Total Score:	

Exploring Multiplication

 Write a multiplication story to answer each question.

ON YOUR OWN

1.

How many juice boxes are there?

2.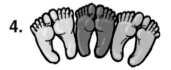

How many legs are there?

3.

How many stamps are there?

4.

How many toes are there?

5.

How many legs are there?

6.

How many birds are there?

Draw pictures of equal groups and arrays for each multiplication story.

7. 4×7 **8.** 1×6 **9.** 8×2

10. 5×9 **11.** 4×4 **12.** 7×1

13. *My Journal:* How do you know when to use multiplication?

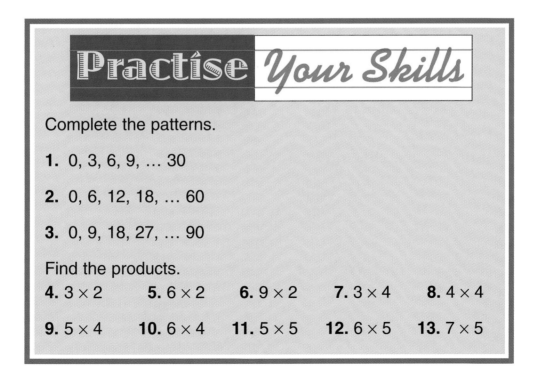

Practise Your Skills

Complete the patterns.

1. 0, 3, 6, 9, … 30

2. 0, 6, 12, 18, … 60

3. 0, 9, 18, 27, … 90

Find the products.

4. 3×2 **5.** 6×2 **6.** 9×2 **7.** 3×4 **8.** 4×4

9. 5×4 **10.** 6×4 **11.** 5×5 **12.** 6×5 **13.** 7×5

Multiplication and Division

Fill in each cell of your multiplication chart.

×	0	1	2	3	4	5	6	7	8	9
0	0 × 0 = 0	0 × 1 = 0								
1	1 × 0 = 0									
2										
3										
4					4 × 4 = 16					
5										
6										
7										
8										
9										

▶ What division facts can you write to go with the multiplication facts?

▶ What patterns can you find in your multiplication chart?

Words to Know

product: the result of multiplying numbers
4 × 3 = (12 ← product)

quotient: the result of dividing one number by another
12 ÷ 4 = (3 ← quotient)

Aladdin's Areas

Advertisements often refer to a typical rug as 3 m by 4 m. What they mean is the rug's length is about 4 m and its width is about 3 m. If you draw a scale drawing of the rug on grid paper, you can easily find the area of the rug.

1 Another popular rug size is about 2 m by 3 m. Draw a rectangle on grid paper to find its area.

2 A large rug is about 4 m by 5 m. Draw a rectangle on grid paper for it and find the area.

3 Some of the most beautiful oriental rugs, although rectangular, have somewhat unusual sizes. How would you find the area of an oriental rug that measures 150 cm by 200 cm? Draw a diagram on grid paper.

4 Make a drawing of a rug you like on grid paper. Label its length and width, then find its area. Add any designs you like.

Exploring Division

▶ Suppose four children found 50¢ on their way to school.
How could they share the money fairly?

▶ Can 50¢ be shared equally by two children with no money left over?
by three children? by five children?
Find all the numbers of children that can share 50¢ equally with no
money left over.

▶ Suppose 50¢ was divided into piles of 12¢ each.
How many piles would there be?
Would any money be left over?

1. Reggie collected 45 bottles. How many empty cartons can he fill?

2. Martina collected 73 bottles. How many empty cartons can she fill?

3. Berta filled six cartons and has two bottles left over. How many bottles did she collect?

4. *My Journal:* How do you know when to use division?

Practise Your Skills

Complete the patterns.

1. 20, 18, 16, ... 0

2. 40, 36, 32, ... 0

3. 60, 54, 48, ... 0

Write each division expression using $)\overline{}$. Then divide.

4. 21 ÷ 3   **5.** 24 ÷ 3   **6.** 27 ÷ 3   **7.** 36 ÷ 4   **8.** 36 ÷ 9

9. 28 ÷ 4   **10.** 16 ÷ 4   **11.** 50 ÷ 5   **12.** 60 ÷ 10   **13.** 54 ÷ 6

Strategies for Multiplication and Division Facts

▶ What is each student doing?

Chalkboard Talk

7 × 7
7 + 7 + 7 + 7 + 7 + 7 + 7 =

7 × 7
5 × 7 = 35
2 × 7 = 14
35 + 14 = 49

Chalkboard Talk

48 ÷ 6
6 + 6 + 6 + 6 + 6
6 + 6 + 6
5 sixes = 30
3 sixes = 18
8 sixes

48 ÷ 6
6 × 8 = 48
48 ÷ 6 = 8

ON YOUR OWN

Find each product or quotient.
Some you may have memorized.
Write or draw pictures to explain the
strategy you used to find the
answers you didn't know.

1. 7 x 8   **2.** 9 x 8   **3.** 5 x 5

4. 6 x 4   **5.** 8 x 3   **6.** 4 x 7

7. 81 ÷ 9   **8.** 63 ÷ 7   **9.** 56 ÷ 8

10. 36 ÷ 6   **11.** 48 ÷ 6   **12.** 21 ÷ 3

13. *My Journal:* How do you decide on a way to find
answers for multiplication and division facts?

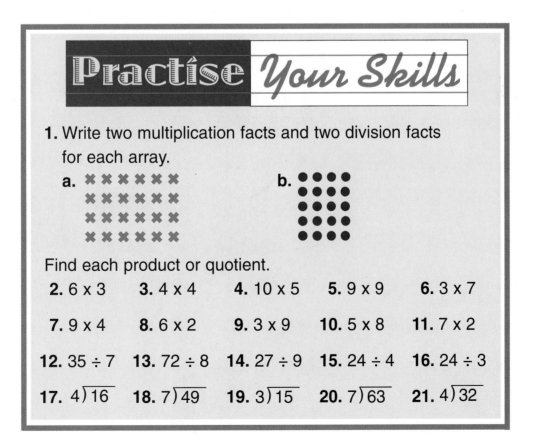

Practîse Your Skills

1. Write two multiplication facts and two division facts
for each array.

a. ✕ ✕ ✕ ✕ ✕ ✕
✕ ✕ ✕ ✕ ✕ ✕
✕ ✕ ✕ ✕ ✕ ✕
✕ ✕ ✕ ✕ ✕ ✕

b. ● ● ● ● ●
● ● ● ● ●
● ● ● ● ●
● ● ● ● ●

Find each product or quotient.

2. 6 x 3   **3.** 4 x 4   **4.** 10 x 5   **5.** 9 x 9   **6.** 3 x 7

7. 9 x 4   **8.** 6 x 2   **9.** 3 x 9   **10.** 5 x 8   **11.** 7 x 2

12. 35 ÷ 7   **13.** 72 ÷ 8   **14.** 27 ÷ 9   **15.** 24 ÷ 4   **16.** 24 ÷ 3

17. 4)‾16‾   **18.** 7)‾49‾   **19.** 3)‾15‾   **20.** 7)‾63‾   **21.** 4)‾32‾

Choosing the Operation

- A school bus holds 60 people. How many buses will be needed to take 240 students and 30 supervisors to the zoo?

- Each seat on a bus holds three people. How many seats are there on a bus?

- The zoo has a rule that there must be an adult supervisor for every eight students. How many supervisors would be needed for your class?

- Suppose you had $4.00 to spend for lunch. What would you buy? How much would your lunch cost? How much change would you get?

SNACK BAR

MENU
Pizza Special $0.99/slice
Sandwiches $1.50
Yogurt $0.75
Muffins $0.75
Fruit $0.50
Ice Cream $1.00
Juice $0.75
Pop $0.85
Milk $0.65

SOUVENI

KEYCHAINS
BOOKS
POSTERS
STE
ANIM
STICK

ADMISSION
ADULTS $4.00
CHILDREN $2.00

ANIMAL FOOD 2 FOR $0.25

ZOO

STOP STOP STOP

1. How much money would it cost for all the students in your class to get into the zoo?

2. How many cones of animal food could you buy with 75¢?

3. Explain how you can find the answers to the following exercises faster by using mental math than by using paper and pencil or a calculator.
   a. 425 + 375
   b. 56 ÷ 9
   c. 520 − 400
   d. 10 x 3

4. Would you use mental math, paper and pencil, or a calculator to do the following calculations? Explain your reasoning.
   a. 5 x 7
   b. 8615 − 3947
   c. 2003 − 1999
   d. 35 ÷ 5

5. *My Journal:* How do you decide which operation to use?

Practise Your Skills

Choose the operation and solve each question.
1. How many packages of five muffins could you make with 45 muffins?
2. How much money would you make if you sold eight cookies for 10¢ each?
3. How many cookies could you buy for 10¢ each if you had 50¢?
4. How much change would you get if you gave $5.00 for something that cost $3.85?
5. How many items could you buy for $3.45 each if you had $10.00?
6. Which is less expensive: four bagels at 9¢ each or six mini muffins at 7¢ each? how much less?

PARTY LOOT BAGS

$1.25

Jumbo Sidewalk Chalk
Grosses Craies Pour Trottoir

Finest Quality • Non-Toxic • Washable
Meilleure Qualité • Non-Toxique • Lavable

For Ages 3 & Up
Pour Plus de 3 Ans

4 for $1.49

You have $25.00 to spend on loot bags for a party.

- Decide on the number of friends you will invite to your party.
- Choose the items for the loot bags.
- For each item you choose, calculate how many you need to buy and the total cost for that item.
- Make sure your total for all the loot bags does not go over $25.00.
- Write to tell how you used the four operations in planning your loot bags.

Whistles

$0.60

NO. 470 4

MADE IN HONG KONG

$1.99

CRAYONS

2 for $ 1.29

KEY... ...NIQUE
AVEC C... ...NIQUE

CHINA

BRASS PADLOCK
CADENAS LAITON

$0.98

CANADA

CANADA

CANADA

RAINBOW
ERASERS

$1.00

GIANT
INSECTS

3 for
$1.49

MADE IN
CHINA

Babioles
De
Festival

Party
Favors

5 / $1.19

5 WATCHES

1:31

1:20

1:12

9:01

1:11

46023

CRAYONS

CRAYONS

Party Blowers
4 for
$0.50

CheckYOURSELF

Great job! You listed the items for the loot bags. You
calculated all the costs. You stayed within your $25.00
budget. You explained clearly in writing how you used
the four operations in your work.

PROBLEM BANK

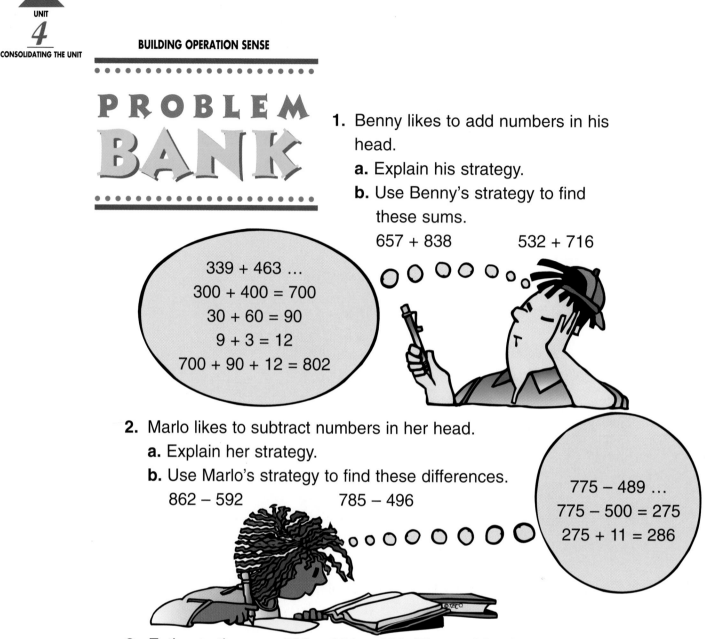

1. Benny likes to add numbers in his head.
   a. Explain his strategy.
   b. Use Benny's strategy to find these sums.

   657 + 838   532 + 716

   339 + 463 ...
   300 + 400 = 700
   30 + 60 = 90
   9 + 3 = 12
   700 + 90 + 12 = 802

2. Marlo likes to subtract numbers in her head.
   a. Explain her strategy.
   b. Use Marlo's strategy to find these differences.
      862 – 592   785 – 496

      775 – 489 ...
      775 – 500 = 275
      275 + 11 = 286

3. Estimate the sum 586 + 381 + 456. Then add using your own procedures.

4. Estimate the difference between 6285 and 1370. Then subtract using your own procedures.

5. Write a multiplication sentence to show the number of stickers on this sheet.

6. Joanna drew this array to show 9 x 7. She wrote 9 x 7 = 63. Use Joanna's strategy to show these facts.

   a. 8 x 6   **b.** 7 x 8   **c.** 5 x 9

7. Write as many multiplication and division facts as you can for each group of numbers.

   a. 8, 16, 2   **b.** 4, 6, 24   **c.** 72, 9, 8

8. Show the meaning of 3 x 9 in as many ways as you can.

9. Which product is greater? Explain how you know.

   a. 6 x 8 or 6 x 9   **b.** 5 x 9 or 9 x 6   **c.** 8 x 7 or 9 x 8

10. A bottle of juice holds enough to fill six glasses. How many bottles would be needed to serve 25 people?

11. There were 22 children at a party. Each child ate one hamburger and drank one juice box. Answer these questions and explain each.

    a. How many packages of four hamburgers were needed?
    b. How many packages of eight buns were needed?
    c. How many three-packs of juice were needed?

12. There are 73 children signed up for gymnastics. How many teams of 8 will there be? Show how you figured out the answer.

Add. Do only those questions with sums greater than 1000.

1. 869	**2.** 765	**3.** 804	**4.** 309	**5.** 3428
+ 128	+ 796	+ 436	+ 540	+ 2681

Subtract. Do only those questions with differences greater than 300.

6. 587	**7.** 707	**8.** 539	**9.** 4276	**10.** 5627
− 450	− 386	− 53	− 3217	− 1256

11. Draw a picture for each.

  a. 5 x 6   **b.** 6 x 3   **c.** 9 x 5   **d.** 3 x 7

12. Complete each sentence in as many ways as you can.

  a. ■ x ■ = 24   **b.** ■ x ■ = 36   **c.** ■ x ■ = 18   **d.** ■ x ■ = 54

  e. 16 ÷ ■ = ■   **f.** 40 ÷ ■ = ■   **g.** 12 ÷ ■ = ■   **h.** 45 ÷ ■ = ■

13. Multiply. Write a related division fact.

  a. 3 x 8   **b.** 7 x 3   **c.** 6 x 4   **d.** 7 x 6   **e.** 9 x 7

  f. 8 x 4   **g.** 4 x 4   **h.** 5 x 7   **i.** 6 x 8   **j.** 7 x 3

14. Divide. Write a related multiplication fact.

  a. 35 ÷ 5   **b.** 40 ÷ 8   **c.** 27 ÷ 3   **d.** 24 ÷ 8   **e.** 15 ÷ 3

  f. 4)36   **g.** 7)42   **h.** 3)9   **i.** 7)56   **j.** 4)28

15. Buns are sold in packages of six.

  a. How many packages would you buy if you needed 50 buns?

  b. How many buns would be in five packages?

16. Pat was born in 1956.

  a. How old would he be now?

  b. In what year will he be 65?

1. Write the numeral for each.
   a. eight hundred forty-three
   b. seven thousand fifty
   c. seven thousand five hundred fifteen
   d. seven thousand four hundred thirty

2. Write each number in words.
   a. 675   **b.** 7463   **c.** 8093   **d.** 19 534

3. Use the digits 0, 5, 7, 3.
   a. Make the greatest number possible.
   b. Make the least number possible.

4. State the value of each underlined digit.
   a. 56<u>8</u>   **b.** 6<u>7</u>32   **c.** <u>7</u>0 426   **d.** 98 4<u>1</u>7

5. Which number is closest to 4000?
   498   4098   3098   3980   4350

6. Order each set of numbers from least to greatest.
   a. 28, 18, 37, 73, 47   **b.** 802, 882, 822, 722, 808
   c. 3874, 3847, 8437, 4738, 4387   **d.** 12 098, 98 021, 98 012, 89 210, 21 098

7. Name each triangle using the terms isosceles, equilateral, right-angled, scalene.

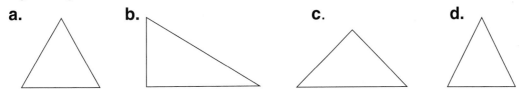

a.   **b.**   **c.**   **d.**

8. Draw four different figures with straight sides. Name them.

107

How can we measure area and perimeter?

EXPLORING AREA AND PERIMETER

S·T·A·R·T·I·N·G
S OUT

4 LITRES
COVERS
40 m²

1 • What measurements had to be taken to decorate this room? List them.

 • Sort the list of measurements you created. What do you notice about them?

 • When do you use perimeter? When do you use area?

 • Make a table like this one to show when each kind of measurement was used to decorate this room.

What Was Measured?	What Kind of Measurement Was It?
Wood for window frame	Perimeter
Rug	Area

Words to Know

Perimeter is the distance around a figure.

Area is the number of square units needed to cover a region.

My Journal: When have you measured area? When have you measured perimeter?

EXPLORING AREA AND PERIMETER
S·T·A·R·T·I·N·G
OUT

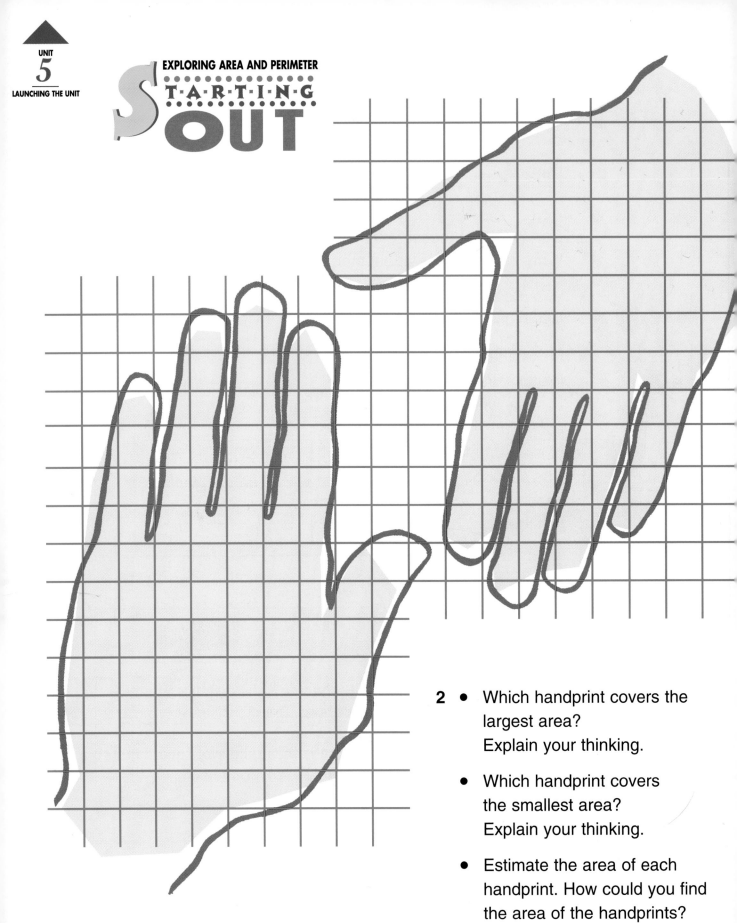

2 • Which handprint covers the largest area? Explain your thinking.

• Which handprint covers the smallest area? Explain your thinking.

• Estimate the area of each handprint. How could you find the area of the handprints?

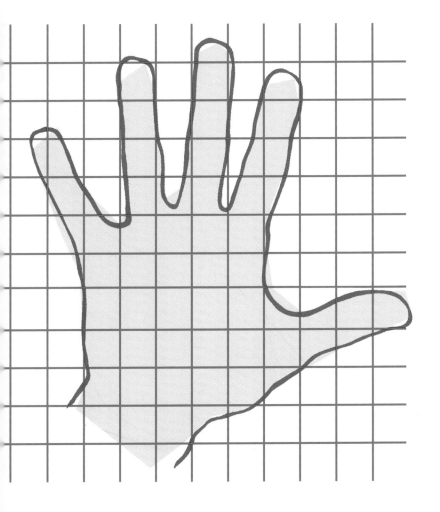

- Trace your hand onto a piece of centimetre grid paper. How does the area of your handprint compare with the areas of the handprints of your classmates?

- How can you find the perimeter of each of these handprints, and your own?

My Journal: What do you notice about area and perimeter? What questions do you have?

UNIT
5
ACTIVITY
1

Exploring Perimeter

▶ Notice the edges of the polygons.
Designs like these are ALLOWED.

▶ Notice the edges of the polygons.
Designs like these are NOT ALLOWED.

114

Different Perimeters, Same Area

▶ Cut a rectangle into four different *polygons* — pieces with straight sides.

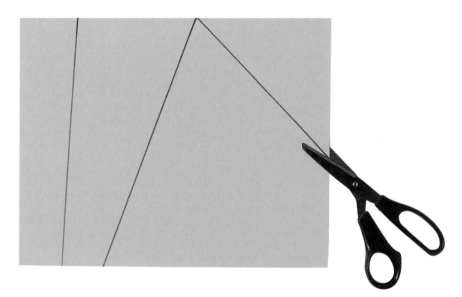

Rearrange the pieces into a new figure.

Find the perimeter.
Remember, *perimeter* is the distance <u>around</u> the figure.

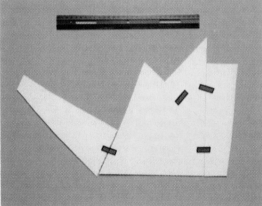

115

ON
YOUR
OWN

ALLOWED   **NOT ALLOWED**

1. Use three same-size squares. Follow the rule above. Rearrange the squares in as many different ways as you can. Find the perimeter for each arrangement.

2. Can you use four squares to follow the rule to make a figure with a perimeter greater than 8 units? Explain your thinking. Draw pictures to show your solutions. The perimeter of the figure shown is 8 units.

3. How many arrangements of four squares have a perimeter of 10 units? Draw these arrangements.

4. *My Journal:* What did you learn that is new in this activity?

Practise Your Skills

1. Find the perimeter of each figure.

   A   B   C

2. Draw a square with a perimeter of 12 cm.

Exploring Area

A

▶ Area = 20 square units

B

▶ Area = 12 square units

Practise Your Skills

1. Draw each figure on dot paper. Make each with an area of 16 square units.
   a. a rectangle   b. a square
   c. a six-sided figure

2. Find the perimeter of each figure in Problem 1.

▶ What is the area of each figure?
How can you calculate it?

1.

2.

3.

ON YOUR OWN

▶ Find the area of each figure.

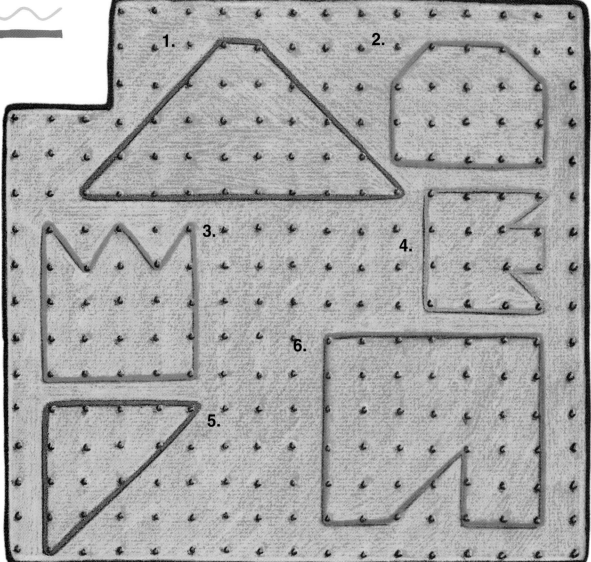

7. Get a piece of dot paper. On it, make any figure you like, as long as it has straight sides. Find the area of your figure. Be prepared to explain how you did it.

8. *My Journal:* Which problem on this page was easiest? Explain.

Long or Tall

Houses

The longhouse was a barrel-roofed house on a rectangular base. The Iroquois called themselves the *Haudenosaunee*, meaning "People of the Longhouse."

Have you ever wondered how people decide on the sizes of their homes? One factor that is considered is the number of people that are going to live there. The Iroquois people of North America frequently built homes shared by many families. These homes were called longhouses. Each family had some private space, but hallways and fireplaces were shared.

The table at the right shows some typical dimensions of floors of longhouses.

Length (metres)	Width (metres)
15	5
23	5.5
30	6
46	6.5

1 Find the area and perimeter of the floor of each longhouse. Which would you expect to be used by the largest number of families? Suppose the smallest longhouse held two families. How many would you expect the largest to hold?

2 Today's apartment buildings or "tall houses" have private areas for families and some common areas. Tell how you think these buildings are like and how they differ from longhouses.

3 What private areas does your class have? What school areas are shared? Find the dimensions, areas, and perimeters of the floors of some of these. Explain why you think they are the size they are.

4 Design a home or room with dimensions of your choice. Find the area and perimeter of its floor. Explain why you chose the size you did.

Areas of Right Triangles

▶ How many right triangles with different areas can you make on your geoboard?

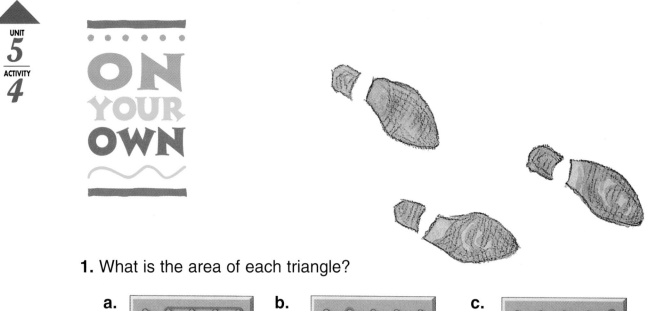

ON
YOUR
OWN

1. What is the area of each triangle?

a. 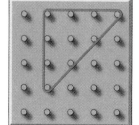   **b.** 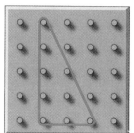   **c.**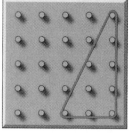

2. Which of the following figures have areas of 2 square units?

a. 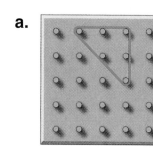   **b.** 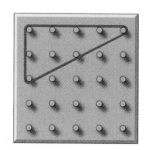   **c.**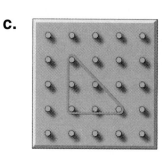

3. Which of these does *not* have an area of 1.5 square units?

a. 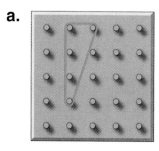   **b.** 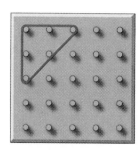   **c.**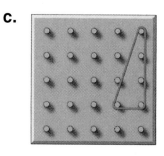

Finding Area in Square Centimetres

- Find objects like this.
- Estimate the area of each in square centimetres.
- Order the objects from least to greatest area according to your estimates.

- Trace the objects.
- Find the area of each in square centimetres.
- Compare your estimates with the calculated areas.

Finding Area in Square Metres

You have 24 m of fencing. You want to build a rectangular pen for your dog.

▶ What is the greatest area you can enclose with that amount of fencing?

Practise Your Skills

On dot paper, draw the following figures. Give each figure an area of 12 square units.

1. a rectangle
2. a parallelogram
3. a hexagon
3. a trapezoid

Explain how you know each figure has an area of 12 square units.

Perimeter = 42 m

Width = 6 m

1. **a.** What is the length of this dog pen?
   b. What is the area?
   c. Stakes are needed every 3 m around the pen to hold up the fence. How many stakes would be needed? Show your solution on grid paper.

2. A tennis court measures 30 m by 20 m.
   a. What is the perimeter?
   b. What is the area?

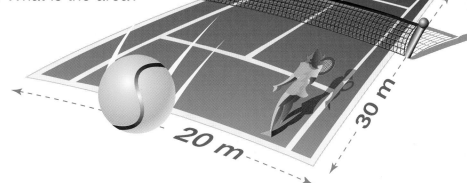

20 m

30 m

3. The area of a volleyball court is about 162 m². The net across the court is about 9 m long. How much tape would you need to mark the outside line around the court?

4. The distance around a skating rink measures 152 m. What do you need to know to find the area of the ice surface?

5. *My Journal:* What did you find out about the rectangular area you can enclose with a given length of fencing?

Go Fly a KITE

Design a Kite

Points to Remember:

- Plan your kite's shape.

- Make a drawing of the kite.

- Find the perimeter.

- Find the area.

- Write clear directions on how to make the kite.

- Check your work.

CheckYOURSELF

Great job! Your kite design and instructions show that you understand the concepts of perimeter and area. Your kite is interesting and attractive and looks like it will fly. You wrote step-by-step instructions accompanied with illustrations that communicated clearly the way to make your kite. You wrote about your use of perimeter and area in your description of your kite's size.

PROBLEM BANK

1. Estimate which figure has the greatest perimeter and which has the smallest perimeter. Check your estimates by measuring.

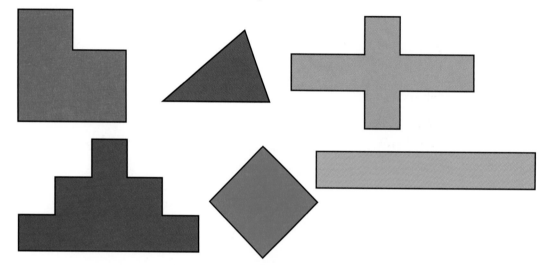

2. Use centimetre grid paper to draw:
   a. a square with a perimeter of 16 cm
   b. a rectangle with a perimeter of 14 cm
   c. two different rectangles, each with a perimeter of 18 cm.

3. A rectangle has one side that is 9 cm long. The perimeter is 42 cm. Use centimetre grid paper to draw the rectangle. Label the lengths of the sides.

4. Use coloured tiles to make five different figures, all with the same perimeter. Each tile must touch another tile completely on at least one side. Copy the figures you made onto grid paper. Record the perimeter of each.

5. Draw three different figures on grid paper. Record the area of each figure in square units. Colour the figure that has the greatest area red, and the one with the smallest area blue.

6. On grid paper, draw:
   a. two figures that have the same area but different perimeters
   b. two figures that have the same perimeter but different areas
   c. two different figures that have the same area and the same perimeter.

7. Make as many different rectangles as you can, each with an area of 20 cm². Which rectangle do you think will have the greatest perimeter? the smallest perimeter? Check your estimates by calculating the perimeter of each rectangle.

8. Draw two different rectangles on grid paper. Make the one with the greater area have the smaller perimeter.

9. Draw two different rectangles on grid paper. Make the one with the smaller area have the greater perimeter.

FROM THIS UNIT

Use dot paper or grid paper for your drawings.

1. Draw a figure with a perimeter of 16 cm.

2. Draw two different rectangles with perimeters of 30 cm.
   What is the area of each?

3. Estimate which figure in each pair has the greater area.
   Then find the area of each.

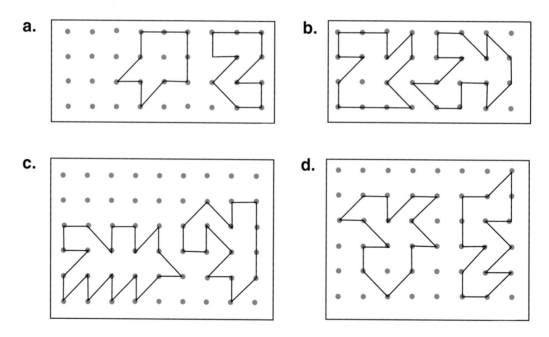

a.

b.

c.

d.

4. Draw a triangle and a square with the same area.

5. Draw two irregular figures with the same area.

6. Draw a rectangle 9 cm long with an area of 27 cm².

S K I L L
BANK
LOOKING BACK

1. Draw a triangle. Is it equilateral, isosceles, or scalene?

2. How are these triangles alike? How are they different?

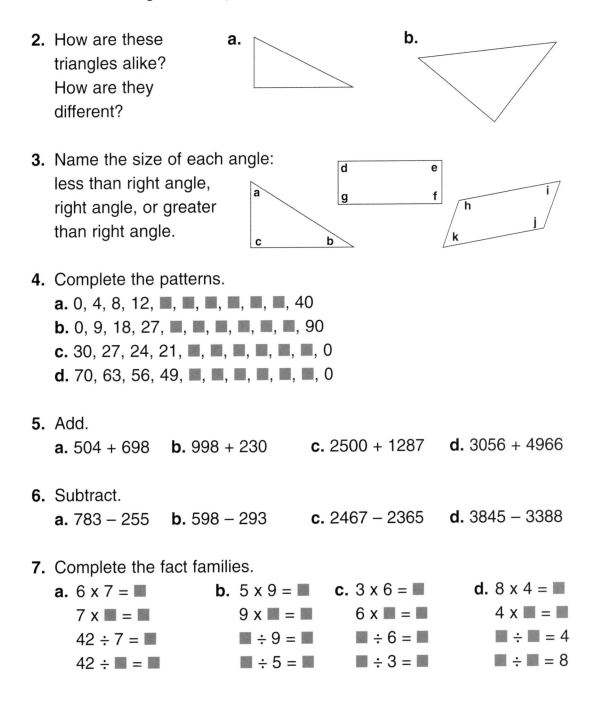

a.

b.

3. Name the size of each angle: less than right angle, right angle, or greater than right angle.

4. Complete the patterns.
   a. 0, 4, 8, 12, ■, ■, ■, ■, ■, ■, 40
   b. 0, 9, 18, 27, ■, ■, ■, ■, ■, ■, 90
   c. 30, 27, 24, 21, ■, ■, ■, ■, ■, ■, 0
   d. 70, 63, 56, 49, ■, ■, ■, ■, ■, ■, 0

5. Add.
   a. 504 + 698   **b.** 998 + 230   **c.** 2500 + 1287   **d.** 3056 + 4966

6. Subtract.
   a. 783 − 255   **b.** 598 − 293   **c.** 2467 − 2365   **d.** 3845 − 3388

7. Complete the fact families.
   a. 6 x 7 = ■   **b.** 5 x 9 = ■   **c.** 3 x 6 = ■   **d.** 8 x 4 = ■
      7 x ■ = ■   9 x ■ = ■   6 x ■ = ■   4 x ■ = ■
     42 ÷ 7 = ■   ■ ÷ 9 = ■   ■ ÷ 6 = ■   ■ ÷ ■ = 4
     42 ÷ ■ = ■   ■ ÷ 5 = ■   ■ ÷ 3 = ■   ■ ÷ ■ = 8

bananas
1.53 kg @ $0.69/kg   1.06
beans
1.12 kg @ $2.18/kg   2.44
grapes
2.3 kg @ $2.99/kg   6.88

10

Jays ahead 1½ games

Toronto - The Toronto Blue Jays have
slowly crept ahead of the rest of the

pack in The American League's
division.

20 CANADA

*H*ow can we
use fractions
and decimals?

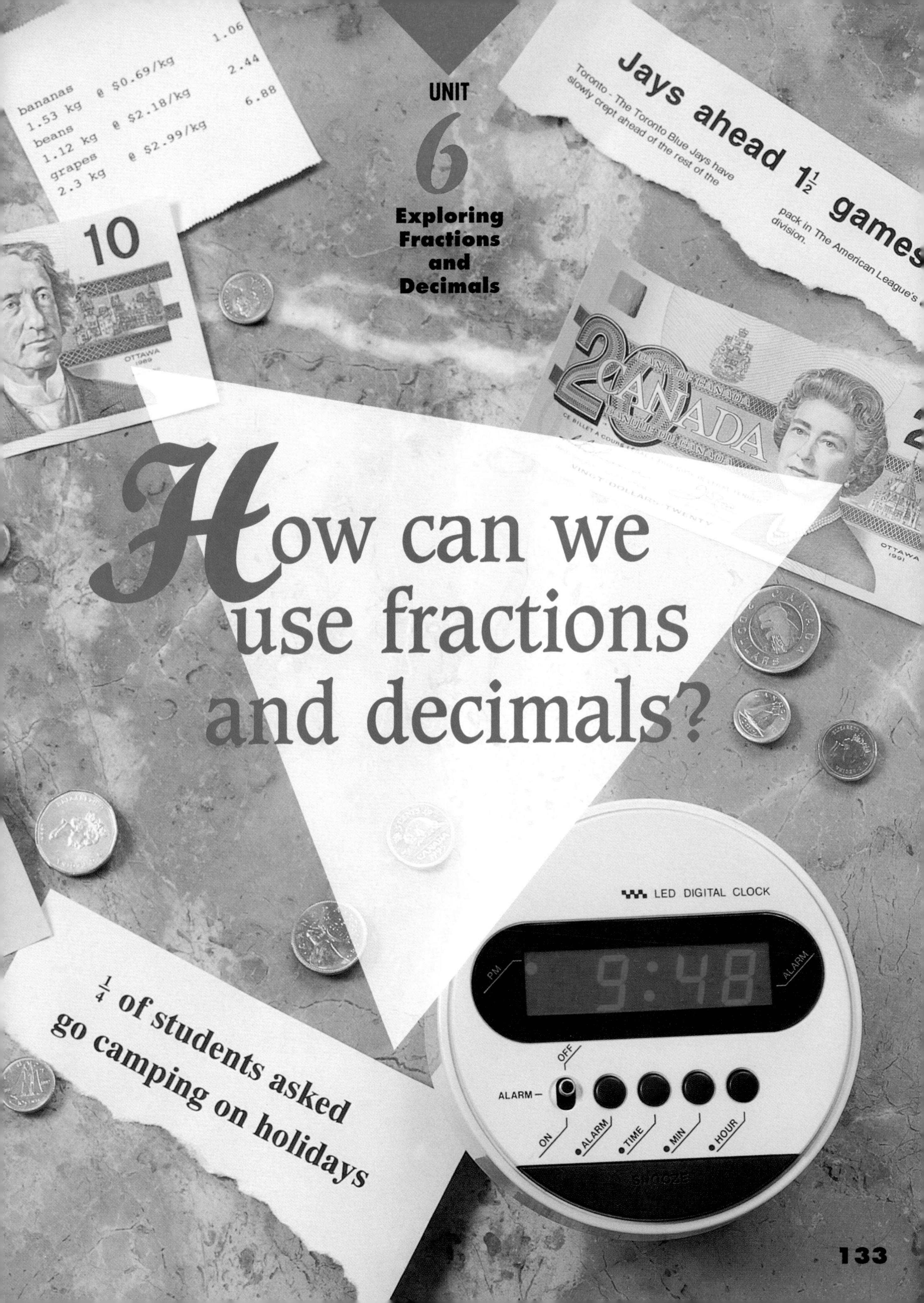

¼ **of students asked
go camping on holidays**

LED DIGITAL CLOCK

PM   *9:48*   ALARM

OFF
ALARM —
ON   ALARM   TIME   MIN   HOUR

EXPLORING FRACTIONS
AND DECIMALS

S·T·A·R·T·I·N·G OUT

Fruit Salad

B. Spurll

1 • How would you write a recipe for fruit salad and s'mores, using the ingredients pictured here?

• If your recipe is for one serving, how would you write that recipe for two servings? for four servings?

• How would the recipe change as you made it for more and more servings? Explain.

• When in your recipe did you use whole numbers?

• When in your recipe did you use fractions?

• Create your own recipe, using fractions, for something you like to eat.

My Journal: At what other times do you use fractions?

S'mores

EXPLORING FRACTIONS
AND DECIMALS

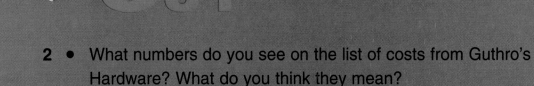

2 • What numbers do you see on the list of costs from Guthro's Hardware? What do you think they mean?

• Where else on the page do you see numbers like those?

• How could you express some of the numbers you see in a different way?

• When else have you seen decimal numbers? When else have you seen fractions?

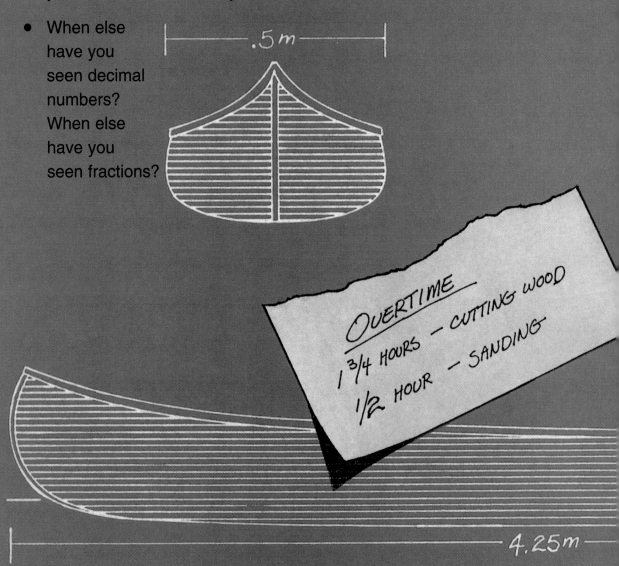

.5 m

OVERTIME

1 3/4 HOURS — CUTTING WOOD

1/2 HOUR — SANDING

4.25m

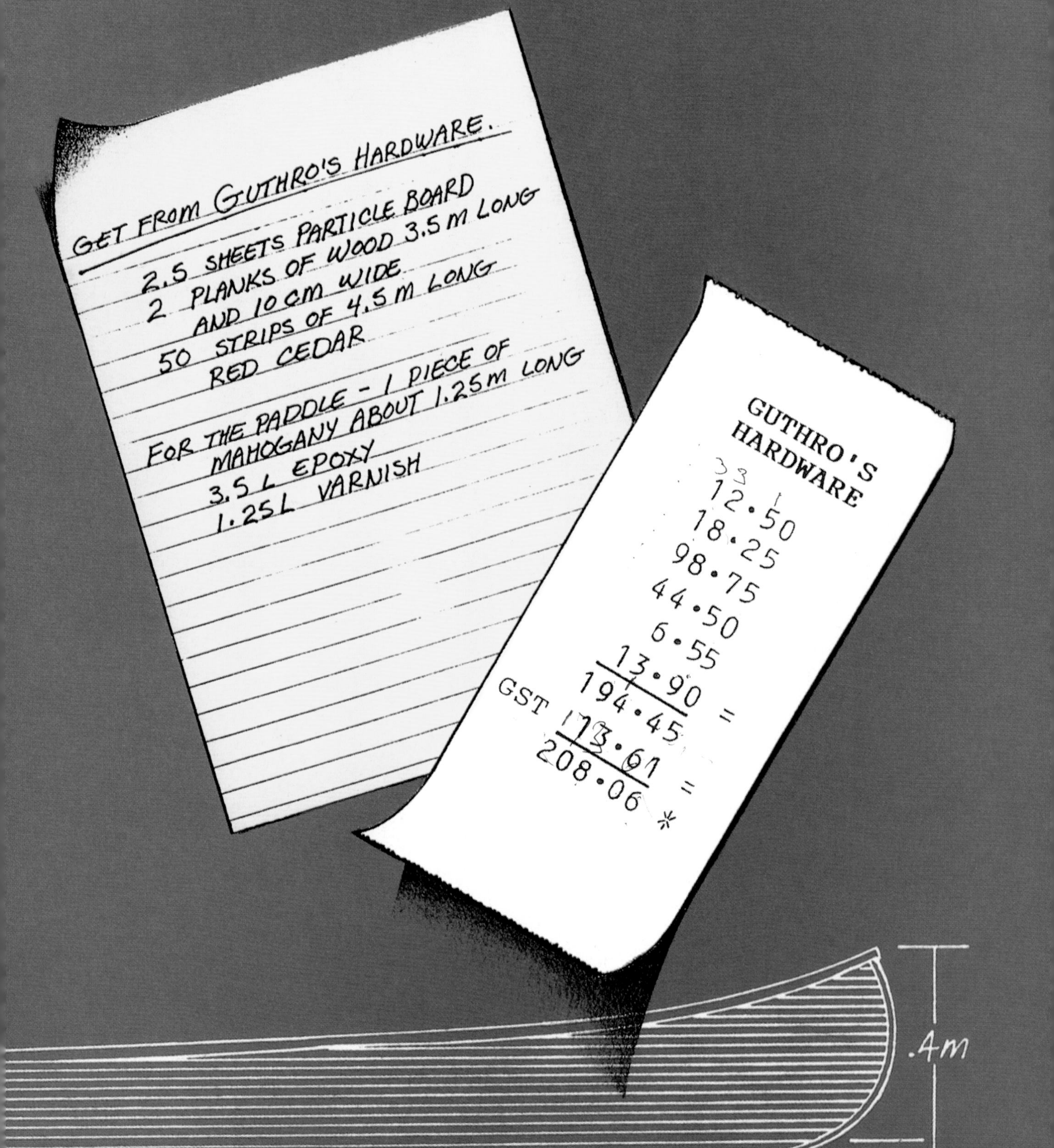

GET FROM GUTHRO'S HARDWARE.

2.5 SHEETS PARTICLE BOARD
2 PLANKS OF WOOD 3.5 m LONG
   AND 10 cm WIDE
50 STRIPS OF 4.5 m LONG
   RED CEDAR

FOR THE PADDLE - 1 PIECE OF
   MAHOGANY ABOUT 1.25 m LONG
3.5 L EPOXY
1.25 L VARNISH

GUTHRO'S
HARDWARE
33
12·50
18·25
98·75
44·50
6·55
13·90 =
194·45
GST 13·61
208·06 *

.4m

My Journal: How do you think fractions and decimals are alike?
How do you think fractions and decimals are different?

Exploring Fractions

▶ What is the area of each part?

May I have the bigger half?

▶ What is the area of each part?

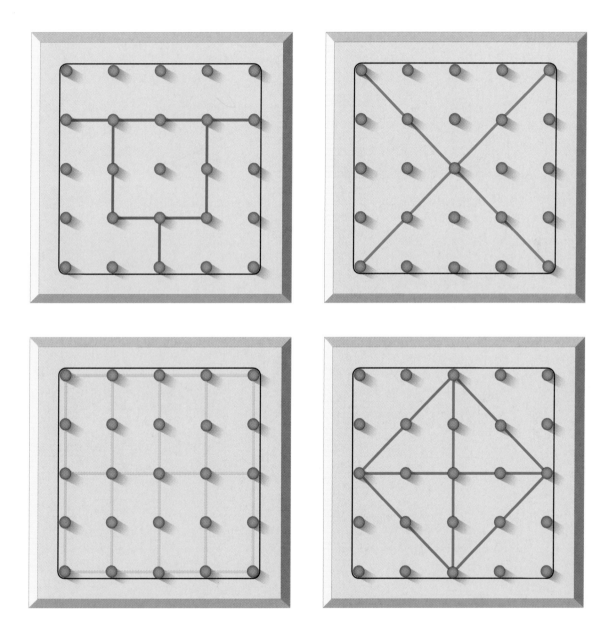

ON YOUR OWN

▶ Estimate the fractional part of the whole each colour section is on each flag.

▶ Name the section by its colour and write the fraction.

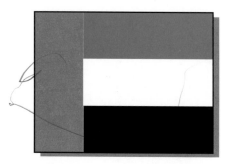

1. Ecuador

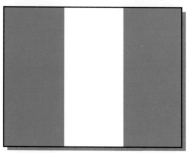

2. United Arab Emirates

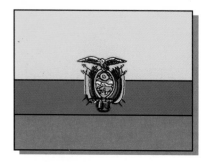

3. Indonesia

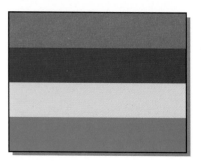

4. Papua New Guinea

5. Ethiopia

6. Nigeria

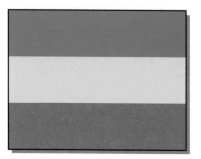

7. Mauritius

8. Panama

9. Which figures do **not** show halves?

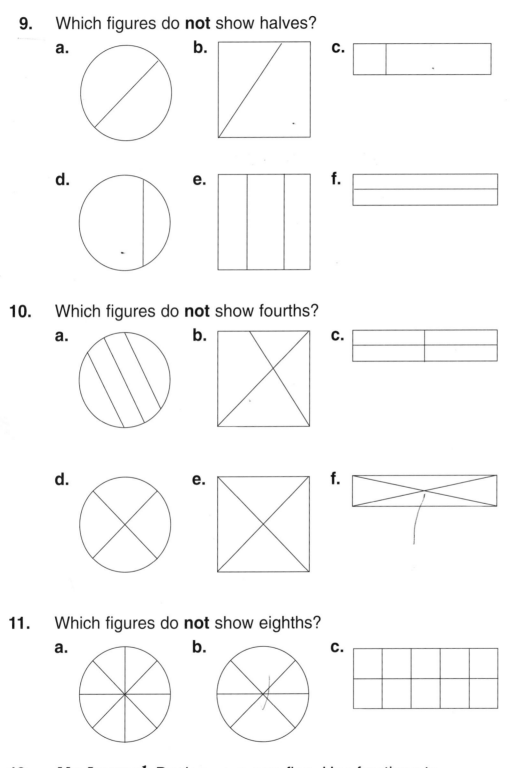

a.

b.

c.

d.

e.

f.

10. Which figures do **not** show fourths?

a.

b.

c.

d.

e.

f.

11. Which figures do **not** show eighths?

a.

b.

c.

12. *My Journal:* Design your own flag. Use fractions to describe its coloured sections. Tell what is important to you about your flag.

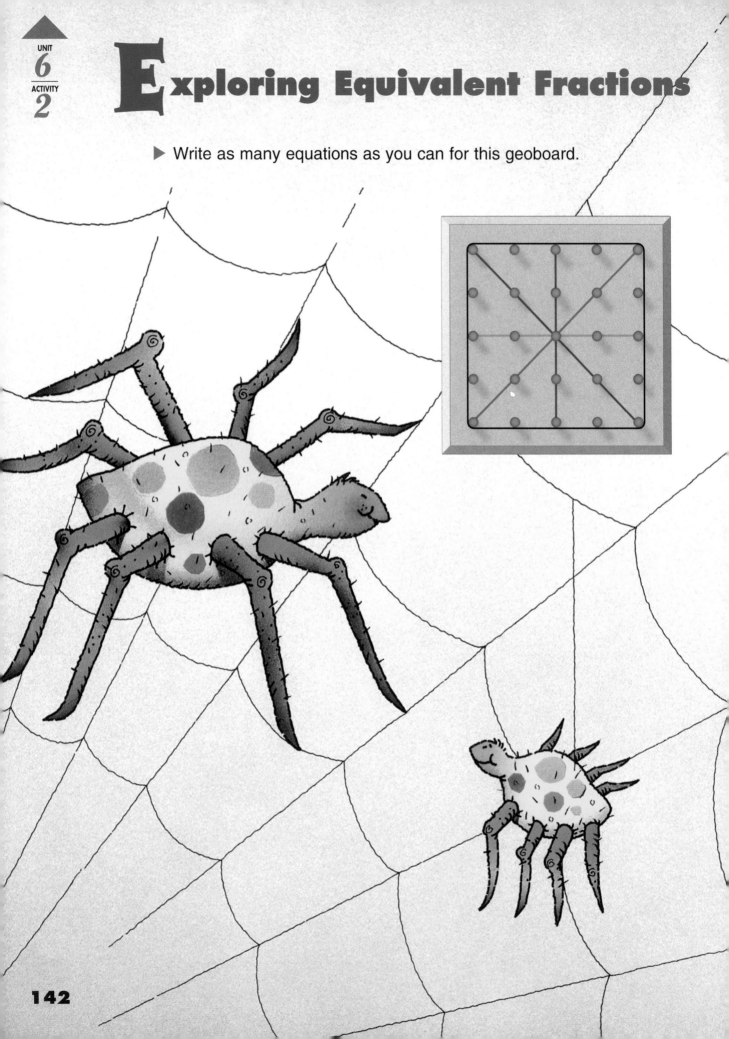

Exploring Equivalent Fractions

▶ Write as many equations as you can for this geoboard.

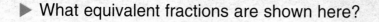

▶ What equivalent fractions are shown here?

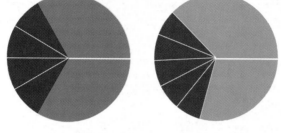

▶ What are the next three fractions equivalent to $\frac{1}{3}$?
How did you decide?

WANTED

$\frac{1}{3}$

ALSO KNOWN AS

$\frac{2}{6}$ $\frac{3}{9}$ $\frac{4}{12}$

143

ON YOUR OWN

1. A lasagna is divided into four equal pieces. Two pieces have been eaten.

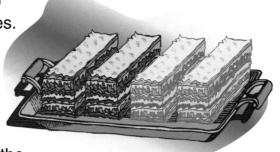

   a. What fraction of the lasagna has been eaten? Name the fraction in two ways.

   b. What fraction of the lasagna is left? Name the fraction in two ways.

   c. Draw a picture of the lasagna. Divide it into smaller equal pieces. Name the fraction that has been eaten. Name the fraction that is left.

2. Some VCRs provide an arrow that helps you estimate how much of a video has played. When a video starts, the arrow is at 0. By the time the video ends, the arrow is at 1. Estimate what fraction of each line the arrow has reached. Name each fraction in two ways.

   a. 0 ──────────────────── 1

   b. 0 ──────────────────── 1

   c. 0 ──────────────────── 1

   d. 0 ──────────────────── 1

3. *My Journal:* What did you learn about equivalent fractions? How can you explain what they are to someone who does not know about them? Use diagrams if you wish.

Practise Your Skills

Complete the fraction equations.

1. $\frac{1}{2} = \frac{\blacksquare}{\blacksquare}$

2. $\frac{1}{5} = \frac{\blacksquare}{\blacksquare}$

3. $\frac{1}{2} = \frac{\blacksquare}{\blacksquare}$

4. $\frac{4}{10} = \frac{\blacksquare}{\blacksquare}$

5. $\frac{\blacksquare}{\blacksquare} = \frac{\blacksquare}{\blacksquare}$

6. $\frac{\blacksquare}{\blacksquare} = \frac{\blacksquare}{\blacksquare}$

Comparing Fractions

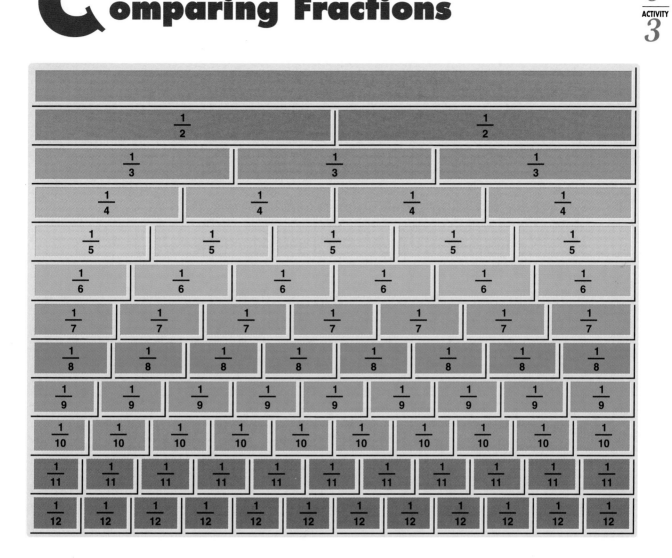

1. Name three fractions from these fraction strips.
   Compare each to one-fourth.

2. What other fractions can you compare?

▶ Use the fraction strips on page 145 to help you solve problems 1 to 3.

1. Make up five questions about comparing fractions. For example, "What are the names of three fractions greater than $\frac{1}{3}$?"

2. Find at least six fractions greater than $\frac{2}{3}$ but less than $\frac{9}{10}$.

3. Put these fractions in order from greatest to least:
$\frac{1}{5}, \frac{1}{2}, \frac{3}{10}, \frac{1}{12}, \frac{4}{4}$

4. Can one half ever be greater than one whole? Explain why or why not. Use examples to support your answer.

5. *My Journal:* What do you find easiest about comparing fractions? Why?

Practise Your Skills

Write a fraction for each coloured part.
Circle the fraction that is greater.

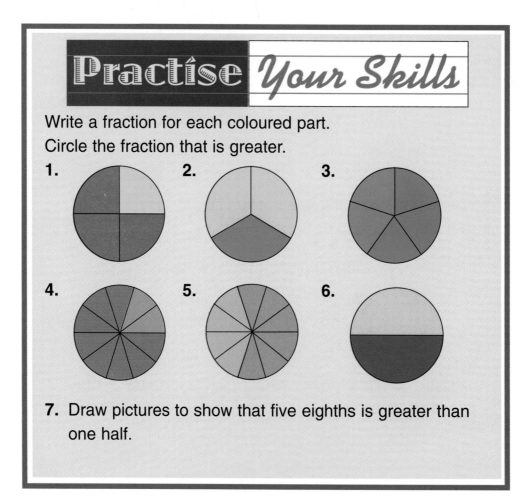

1.

2.

3.

4.

5.

6.

7. Draw pictures to show that five eighths is greater than one half.

Fractions of Sets

▶ What fraction of the pegs on the board are on or inside the triangle?

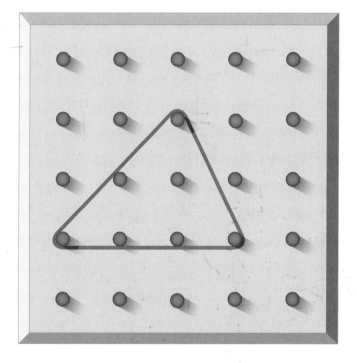

1. What is the maximum number of inside pegs you can get using a triangle? What fraction of the total number of pegs is this?

2. Make a triangle with $\frac{3}{25}$ of the pegs inside. Draw a picture of it.

3. *My Journal:* Do you enjoy geoboard activities? Explain.

FRACTIONS
of the MOON

Have you ever looked up at the moon and used a fraction to describe it? The moon looks like a half-circle about seven days after the new moon. We might call it a half-moon because of the way it looks, but it is a first-quarter moon because it is one quarter of the way through its orbit. It is in the stage of waxing, or showing more of its face. It takes the moon about $29\frac{1}{2}$ days to go through its orbit.

The moon keeps waxing until it is a full moon. Then it starts to wane, or show less of its face. It gets to a half-moon again about three weeks after the new moon. Now it is a third-quarter moon, because it is in the third quarter of its orbit. Many people see the waxing and waning of the moon in another way — as though it is gaining and losing weight. For example, the Taulipang people of Guyana believe that each moon is first fed well (waxing), and then starved (waning) by Venus and Jupiter.

1. We call the moon a first-quarter moon about seven or eight days after the new moon. How could you express that number of days as a fraction of the moon's orbit? Explain why that is one quarter.

2. Take some time to observe the moon over a few weeks. Draw the shapes you see and use fractions to describe them. Note when during the 24-hour day you can see the moon.

3. Develop your own method for describing moon phases using fractions. Explain how you chose that method and why you think it is a good one.

1

2

3

4

Fractions of Sets

▶ A recent survey found that 1 out of 4 dog owners
in Canada celebrates his or her dog's birthday.

▶ Of the people who celebrate their dogs' birthdays,
2 out of 5 give the dog a special treat.

1. **a.** What fraction of the masks have feathers?
   b. What fraction of the masks cover the whole face?
   c. What fraction of the masks cover the eye area only?

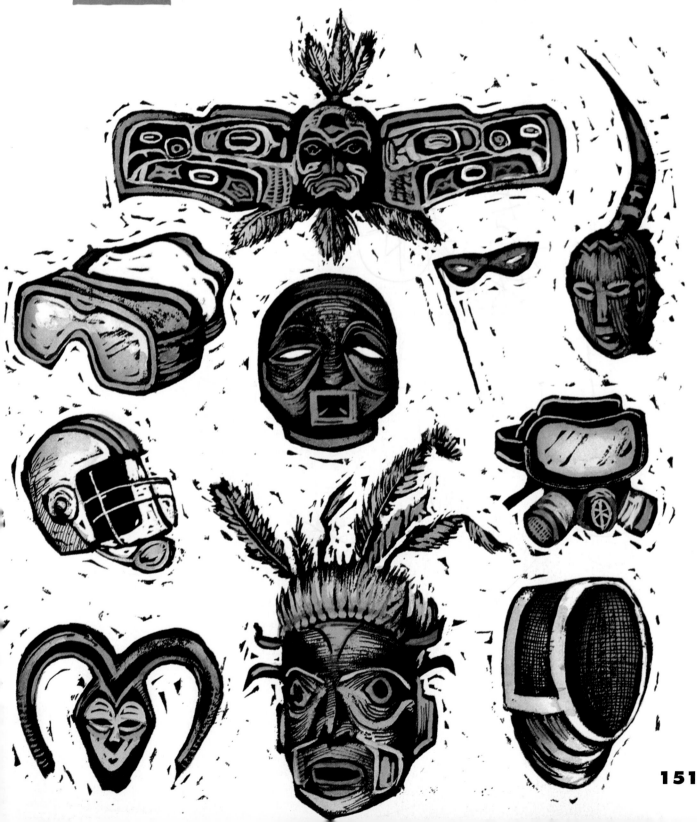

151

2. Think about the people in your household.
   a. What fractional part of your household is male?
   b. What fraction are female?
   c. What fraction of the people in your household are over 18?
   d. What fraction are under 18?

3. *Math* is a word that is $\frac{3}{4}$ consonants and $\frac{1}{4}$ vowels.
   a. Think of three other words you can describe as $\frac{3}{4}$ consonants and $\frac{1}{4}$ vowels.
   b. Think of some words that are $\frac{3}{5}$ consonants and $\frac{2}{5}$ vowels.
   c. How would you describe your own name using fractions?

4. *My Journal:* What have you learned about fractional parts of sets? Explain.

Practise Your Skills

1. a. Draw five people so that:
      two fifths are wearing hats;
      one fifth is wearing boots; and
      four fifths have short hair.
   b. Use a fraction to describe something else about the group.

2. a. What fraction of the crackers are on each plate?
   b. What fraction of the crackers are square?
   c. What fraction of the crackers have cheese?
   d. Use a fraction to describe something else about the crackers.

Equivalent Fractions

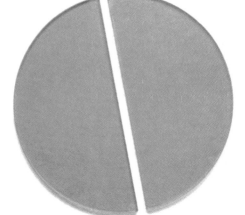

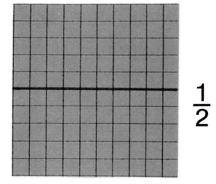

$\dfrac{1}{2}$

▶ What other fraction could you use to describe $\frac{1}{2}$ of the square?

How did you decide?

Could you use other fractions to describe half of each figure?

ON YOUR OWN

1. Divide a 10 x 10 grid into 10 equal sections. Shade three of these sections. Write two equivalent fractions for the shaded region. Explain why you wrote those fractions.

2. Use two 10 x 10 grids. Shade $\frac{4}{10}$ on one grid and $\frac{40}{100}$ on the other. What do you notice about the shaded regions?

3. Which is greater, $\frac{35}{100}$ or $\frac{7}{10}$? Prove your answer using 10 x 10 grids.

Refer to the figure at the right for problems 4 to 8.

4. How many long orange strips are needed to cover the 10 x 10 grid completely? What fraction of the grid does one orange strip represent? How many blue squares are needed? What fraction of the grid does one square represent?

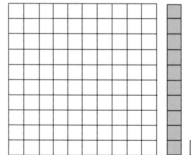

5. How many strips and squares would be needed to show $\frac{38}{100}$?

6. How many ways can you show $\frac{25}{100}$ using orange strips and blue squares? Show each.

7. How could you show eight tenths using orange strips and blue squares?
How could you show eight hundredths?
Write the fractions.

8. Write the fraction shown for each set of strips and squares placed on a 10 x 10 grid.
  a. 3 orange strips, 2 blue squares
  b. 3 orange strips
  c. 2 orange strips, 12 blue squares
  d. 40 blue squares

9. *My Journal:* What have you learned about ways to write fractions?

Practise Your Skills

Name the fraction of each figure that is coloured.
1. 2. 3. 4.
5. 6. 7. 8.
9. 10. 11. 12.

Decimals Equivalent to Fractions

How do decimals and fractions compare?

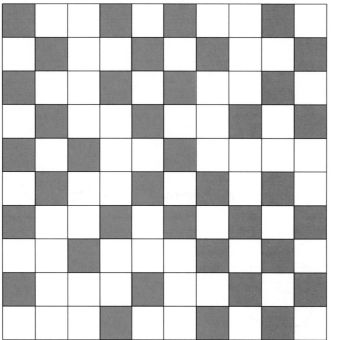

$$\frac{38}{100} = 0.38$$

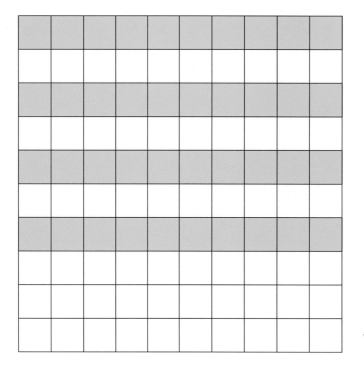

$$\frac{40}{100} = \frac{4}{10} = 0.4$$

156

ON YOUR OWN

1. Name the fractions shown in as many ways as you can.

   a.

   b.

   c.

   d.

2. *My Journal:* How are decimals related to fractions?

Practise Your Skills

1. Write each fraction as a decimal.

   a. $\frac{1}{10}$ **b.** $\frac{5}{10}$ **c.** $\frac{8}{10}$ **d.** $\frac{80}{100}$

   e. $\frac{8}{100}$ **f.** $\frac{26}{100}$ **g.** $\frac{99}{100}$ **h.** $\frac{62}{100}$

2. Write each decimal as a fraction.

   a. 0.40   **b.** 0.04   **c.** 0.4   **d.** 0.44

3. Write each as a fraction and as a decimal.

   a. 7 hundredths   **b.** 28 hundredths

   c. 70 hundredths   **d.** 7 tenths

4. Use 10 x 10 grids to show each number in problem 3.

Decimals Equivalent to Fractions

▶ Can you find decimal equivalents for these fractions?

$\frac{1}{2}$ $\frac{1}{3}$ $\frac{1}{4}$ $\frac{1}{5}$ $\frac{1}{6}$ $\frac{1}{8}$ $\frac{1}{10}$

Ways to Find Decimals Equivalent
to Fractions

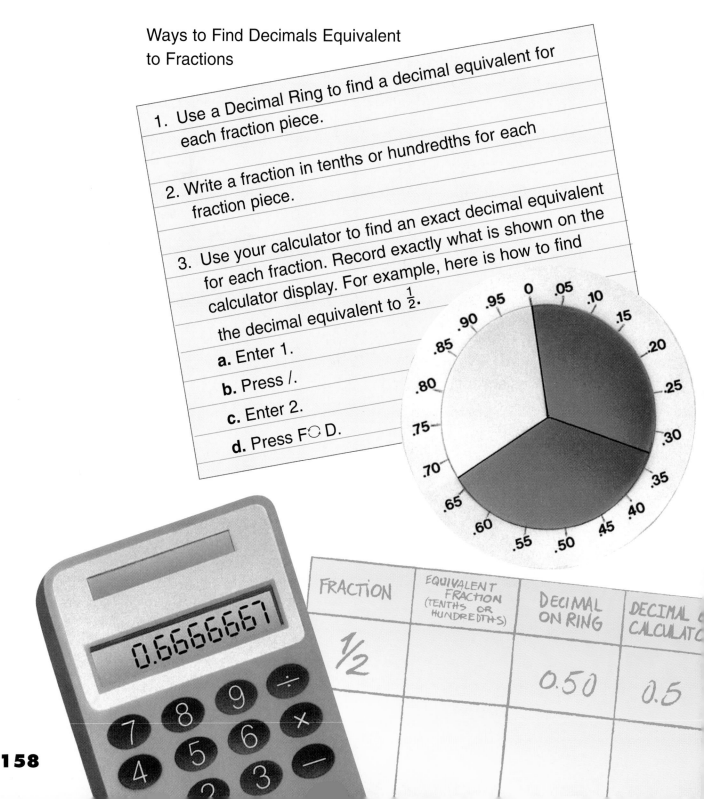

1. Use a Decimal Ring to find a decimal equivalent for each fraction piece.

2. Write a fraction in tenths or hundredths for each fraction piece.

3. Use your calculator to find an exact decimal equivalent for each fraction. Record exactly what is shown on the calculator display. For example, here is how to find the decimal equivalent to $\frac{1}{2}$.

   a. Enter 1.
   b. Press /.
   c. Enter 2.
   d. Press F⊙D.

FRACTION	EQUIVALENT FRACTION (TENTHS OR HUNDREDTHS)	DECIMAL ON RING	DECIMAL C CALCULATO
$\frac{1}{2}$		0.50	0.5

0.6666667

ON YOUR OWN

1. Enter $\frac{2}{5}$ in your calculator. Press the F⌒D key. Then press the F⌒D key again.

   a. Record each calculator display.

   b. Why didn't your last calculator display show $\frac{2}{5}$?

2. Find three fractions whose decimal equivalents fall within each range.

   a. 0 to 0.25   c. 0.51 to 0.75

   b. 0.26 to 0.50   d. 0.76 to 1.00

3. Name a decimal between 0.4 and 0.5.

4. *My Journal:* Explain two ways to find a decimal equivalent to a given fraction. Which is easier for you? Why?

Practise Your Skills

Use any method to find the decimal equivalent for each fraction.

1. $\frac{3}{4}$ 2. $\frac{2}{8}$ 3. $\frac{3}{5}$ 4. $\frac{9}{10}$ 5. $\frac{3}{8}$ 6. $\frac{5}{6}$

7. $\frac{2}{3}$ 8. $\frac{35}{100}$ 9. $\frac{3}{100}$ 10. $\frac{1}{5}$ 11. $\frac{2}{10}$ 12. $\frac{25}{100}$

Make a Two - Loop Glider

Here's what to do:

1. Cut one strip of paper 2 cm wide and 16 cm long.
2. Cut another strip 1.5 cm wide and 14 cm long.
3. For each strip, bring the ends together to form a loop. Overlap the ends and tape them together on both sides.
4. Line up one end of the straw with the edge of the wider loop. Tape the straw to the inside of the loop, on the overlap, to form the back loop of the glider.
5. Put the narrower loop on the other end of the straw. Place the loop so that about $\frac{1}{8}$ of the straw sticks out past the front edge of the loop. Tape the straw to the inside of the loop, on the overlap.
6. Make sure that the loops are perpendicular to the straw. If they are even slightly off, adjust the tape. Inspect your glider from all angles to check that it is balanced and symmetrical.

Glider Flying Competition

Plan a Playing Field:

1. Use adding machine tape to establish the total length of the playing field.
2. Establish side boundaries and a starting line.
3. Using the total length of the playing field as one whole, mark off the tape in fractions.

Flying Rules:

1. Your feet must be behind the starting line when you launch your glider.
2. If your glider goes out-of-bounds, you can launch it again.
3. When your glider lands in-bounds, estimate the fraction of the length of the playing field it flew. Use the front of the glider to estimate. Record the actual distance using fractions and decimals.
4. Decide how many turns everyone gets before a winner is declared.

*C*heck**Y**OURSELF

Great job! Your glider is constructed correctly. You followed all the directions in the proper order. After testing, you made some adjustments and then your glider was able to fly farther. You used fractions and decimals, and described your work with them correctly.

P R O B L E M
BANK

1.

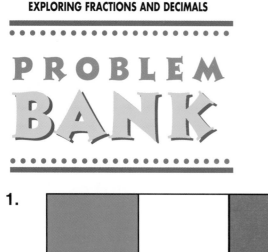

a. Describe this flag using fractions.

b. Design a flag that can be described using the same fractions.

2. A farmer has a field that is $\frac{1}{4}$ corn, $\frac{1}{8}$ hay, $\frac{1}{8}$ alfalfa, and $\frac{1}{2}$ wheat.

a. Draw and label a sketch to show what the field might look like.

b. Write to tell how the parts can be combined to describe the whole field.

3. Complete each of these statements in three ways.

a. $\frac{1}{2}$ is equal to ...

b. $\frac{1}{2}$ is greater than ...

c. $\frac{1}{2}$ is less than ...

4. Use the fraction circles or draw pictures to help you complete these statements.

a. One third is greater than _____

b. One quarter is equal to _____

c. Two thirds is greater than _____

d. Three fourths is less than _____

e. Two thirds is _____ than three quarters

f. Three sixths is _____ one half

5. Think about this group of aliens.

a. What fractional part have two antennae? three antennae? one antenna?

b. What other fractions can you use to describe this set? Write as many as you can, then compare with a friend to find more ideas.

6. Jamal says that $\frac{60}{100}$ is shaded. Sandra says that $\frac{6}{10}$ is shaded. Who do you agree with? Explain.

▶ Use your fraction pieces, Decimal Ring, calculator, or any method you choose to solve problems 7 and 8. Remember to explain your thinking.

7. Melissa ate $\frac{1}{2}$ of her granola bar. Her friend ate 0.50 of hers. Could they have shared one bar? Explain.

8. 25 out of 100 students prefer chocolate ice cream. Franco thinks that is $\frac{1}{4}$ of the students and Tamika thinks it is 0.25 of the students. Can they both be right? Explain.

S K I L L
BANK
FROM THIS UNIT

1. What fraction of the birds are

    a. blue?   **b.** not blue?   **c.** pigeons?   **d.** robins?

2. Cut and colour grid paper to show these fractions.

    a. $\frac{3}{10}$ **b.** $\frac{1}{2}$ **c.** $\frac{3}{4}$ **d.** $\frac{4}{5}$ **e.** $\frac{1}{3}$

3. a. Use fractions to tell about the number of pegs inside of, outside of, and on the edge of the quadrilateral.

    b. What other quadrilaterals can you find that can be described with these same fractions? Draw the ones that you find on Activity Master 15.

4. Colour a design on a 10 x 10 grid. Use fractions to describe the part of the grid covered by each colour.

5. Use a table to sort the fractions.

$\frac{1}{3}$ $\frac{2}{3}$ $\frac{1}{5}$ $\frac{3}{4}$ $\frac{3}{6}$

$\frac{8}{10}$ $\frac{4}{10}$ $\frac{3}{8}$ $\frac{1}{6}$ $\frac{7}{8}$

Closest to 0	Closest to 0.5	Closest to 1

164

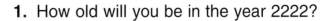

1. How old will you be in the year 2222?

2. Find the difference between 1000 and 687.

3. Find the sum of 5835 and 2417.

4. What is the total of 729 and 1206?

5. How many groups of 3 are in 27?

6. How many groups of 6 are in 30?

7. How many people could share 36 stickers equally?

8. Draw a picture for each multiplication fact. Find each product.
   a. 6 x 3   **b.** 4 x 9   **c.** 3 x 8   **d.** 7 x 6

9. Draw a square with a perimeter of 36 cm. What is the area of the square? Draw a different figure with the same perimeter but different area.

10. Which figures have the same area?

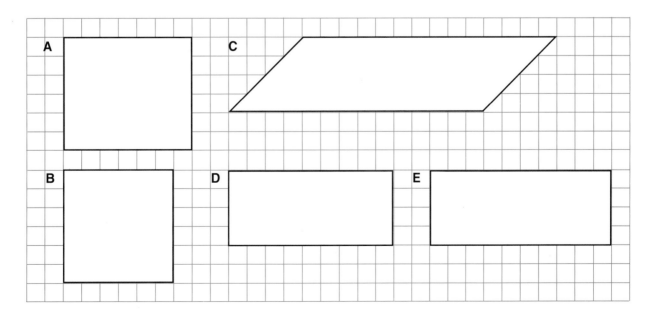

World Records

The record number of table tennis hits
in 60 seconds is 172.

The record number of somersaults performed
on a trampoline is 75 in 1 minute.

The record number of hopscotch games played by
one person in one day is 307.

The record set for bathtub racing
is 145 km in 24 hours.

The record number of footbag kicks
in 5 minutes is 912.

The record speed for opening oysters is 100
in a little over 2 minutes.

The greatest distance covered by a team of leapfroggers
is 1611 km in 10 days.

Hank Aaron holds the record for home runs:
755 during his 22-year career.

The furthest a basketball has been dribbled
is 427 km in 14 days.

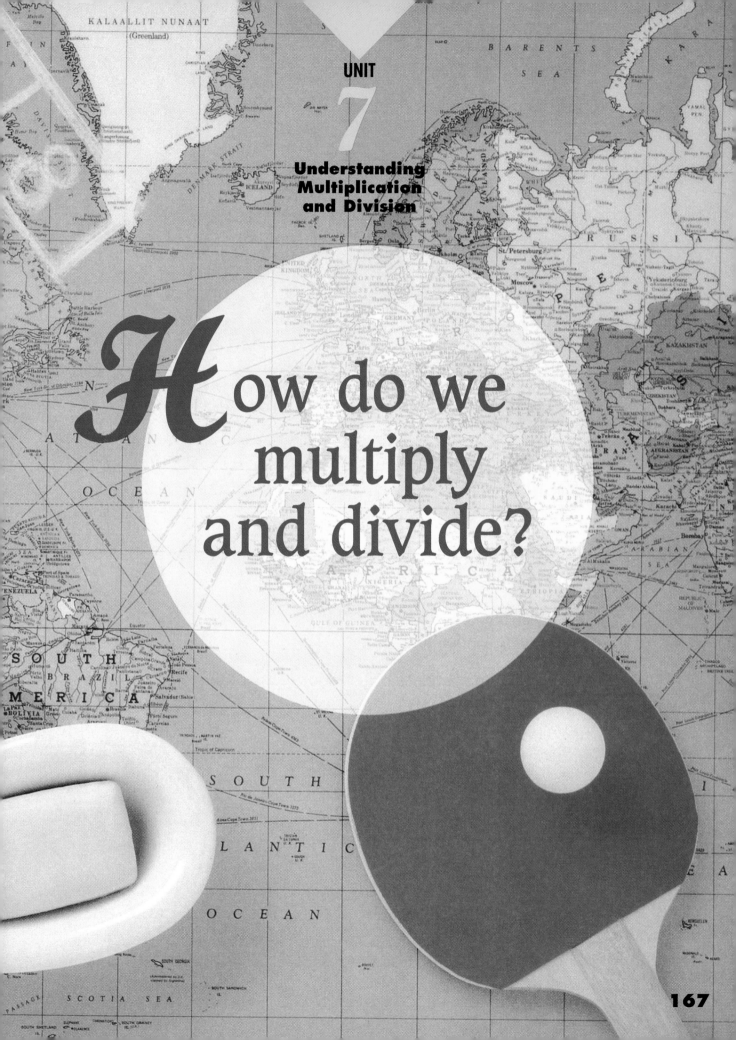

*H*ow do we multiply and divide?

UNDERSTANDING
MULTIPLICATION AND DIVISION

S·T·A·R·T·I·N·G
OUT

1 • What is common about the way things
are arranged in each picture?
• How would each person use
multiplication in her or his job?
• Write story problems for these pictures
that someone could solve using
multiplication or division.

My Journal: When do you use multiplication
and division?

Collecting and Graphing Data

▶ How many cubes can you place on a grid in one minute?

▶ How many times can you write your name in one minute?

Sebastian Sebastian
Sebastian Sebastian
Sebastian Sebastian
Sebastian Sebastian
Sebastian Sebastian
Sebastian

▶ How many times can you write the number 100 in one minute?

100 100 100 100 100 100
100 100 100 100 100 100
100 100 100 100 100 100
100 100 100 100 100 100 100
100 100 100 100 100 100

Take a few minutes to find out! Make a graph to display your data.

▶ Use the data you collected to estimate the number of times you could do each of these tasks in
   • five minutes
   • ten minutes

Multiplying Using Arrays

How many are in the array?

4 rows of 16

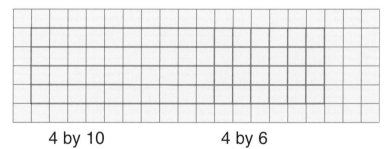

4 rows of 10 and 4 rows of 6

4 by 10   4 by 6

How does your array compare?
How can you find the total?

1. Draw this yard on grid paper. Find the area.

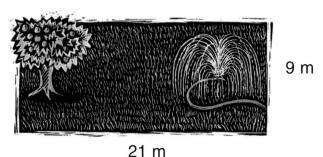

9 m

21 m

2. Write a multiplication sentence to describe the total number of squares in this array.

3. *My Journal:* What did you learn about using arrays to multiply?

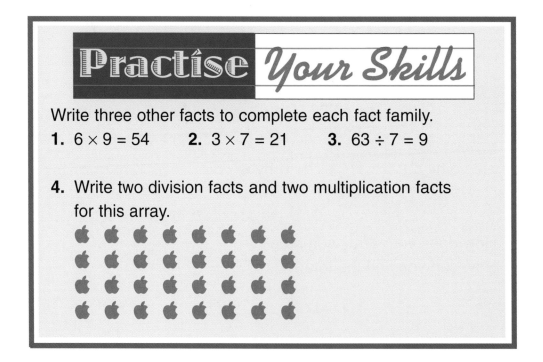

Practise *Your Skills*

Write three other facts to complete each fact family.

1. $6 \times 9 = 54$ **2.** $3 \times 7 = 21$ **3.** $63 \div 7 = 9$

4. Write two division facts and two multiplication facts for this array.

Using Parts of Arrays

Here are tiles to decorate space in a subway station.
8 x 36 tells the number of tiles in this space.

36 tiles

8 tiles

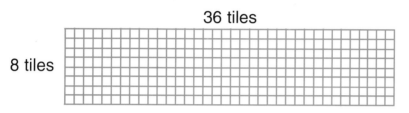

Here the space is filled with coloured tiles.

▶ Write a multiplication sentence for each coloured part.
How can you find the total?

Here is the same space filled another way.

▶ Write a multiplication sentence for each coloured part.
How can you find the total?

173

ARRAY ST.

Lots of tiles are needed to cover some spaces!
This sketch shows plans for a new tiled sign.

▶ About how many tiles are needed?

146 tiles

8 tiles

This sketch shows one way to divide the space.

▶ Write a multiplication sentence for each coloured part.
How can you find the total?

100   40   6

8

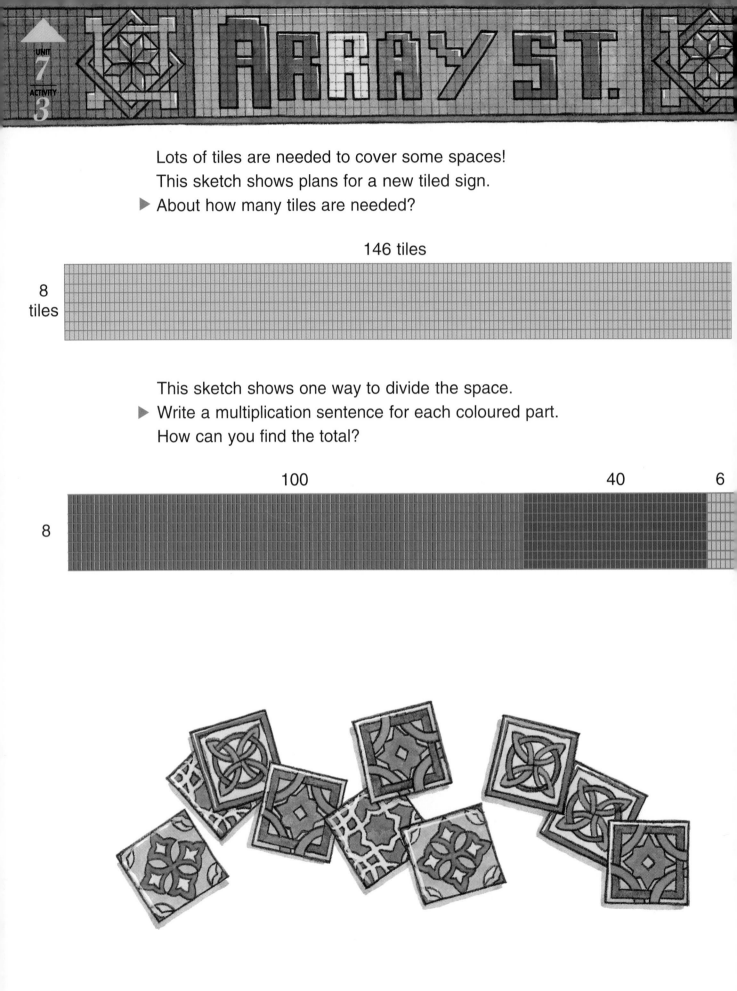

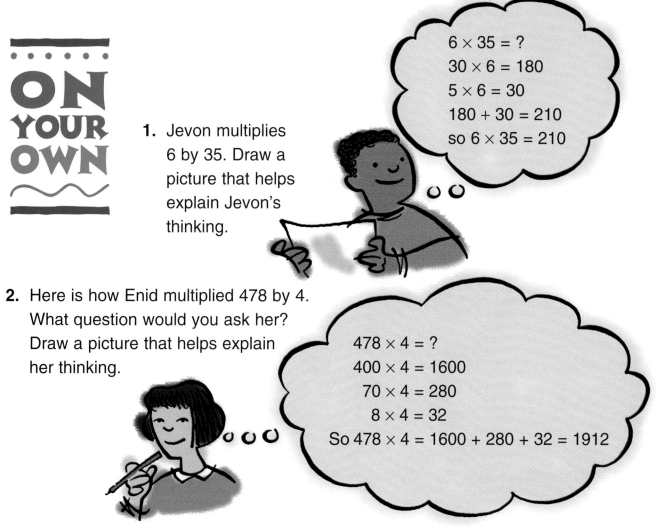

ON YOUR OWN

1. Jevon multiplies 6 by 35. Draw a picture that helps explain Jevon's thinking.

6 × 35 = ?
30 × 6 = 180
5 × 6 = 30
180 + 30 = 210
so 6 × 35 = 210

2. Here is how Enid multiplied 478 by 4. What question would you ask her? Draw a picture that helps explain her thinking.

478 × 4 = ?
400 × 4 = 1600
70 × 4 = 280
8 × 4 = 32
So 478 × 4 = 1600 + 280 + 32 = 1912

3. Imagine a sheet of stamps with 8 rows of 24 stamps. Sketch the array. How can you find the total?

4. *My Journal:* What have you learned about multiplying?

Practise Your Skills

Find the products.

1. 3 × 52
2. 7 × 84
3. 5 × 91
4. 6 × 55

5. 64 × 7
6. 42 × 9
7. 68 × 4
8. 29 × 3

9. 53 × 9
10. 74 × 6
11. 59 × 5
12. 47 × 7

13. 198 × 3
14. 538 × 6
15. 607 × 6
16. 830 × 9

Searching for Patterns

Estimate first. Then work with a partner to solve each problem two ways. Show how you separate each problem into easier steps. Tell about any materials you use.

24 crayons in a box
30 children
24 × 30
How many crayons are there if each child has a box?

48 markers in a box
60 boxes
48 × 60
How many markers are there if the school has 60 boxes?

75 pencils in a box
50 boxes
75 × 50
How many pencils were used if all 50 boxes are empty?

Estimating Products

Celina estimates she will walk between 75 km and 90 km in the next two weeks. About how far does she expect to walk each day?

▶ What is the missing factor?

14 x ? =   Range:
75
|
90

14 x 7 = 98 too high
14 x 5 = 70 too low
14 x 6 = 84

▶ Use estimation to find each missing factor. The product must be within the range.

1.
18 × ? =   Range:
110
|
130

2.
15 × ? =   Range:
290
|
310

3.
45 × ? =   Range:
250
|
300

4.
92 × ? =   Range:
260
|
300

5.
290 × ? =   Range:
1000
|
1200

6.
356 × ? =   Range:
3000
|
3300

The Target Game

Group

2 players

Materials

Each player needs:

• Recording sheet

• Calculator

Each pair needs:

• Score sheet

Goal:

• To get closest to the target number

Game Rules:

1 Each pair chooses a game board from page 179.

2 Each player chooses a number from each column on the game board and records them as factors in a multiplication expression. Once a player records the two numbers they cannot be changed.

3 Each player multiplies his or her two numbers to find the product.

4 Players compare their products to decide whose is closer to the target number on the game board. The player whose product is closer scores a point.

5 If both products are the same or the products are the same number from the target, each player gets a point.

6 Players use calculators to settle any disagreements.

7 Players choose another game board and continue play.

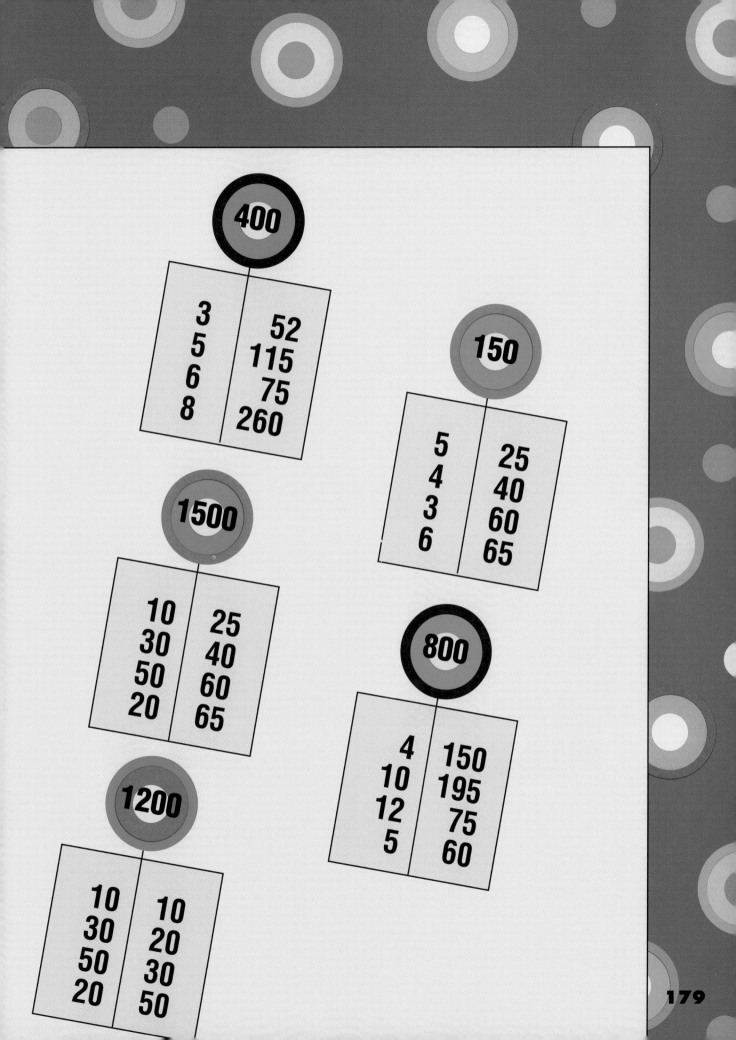

400

3	52
5	115
6	75
8	260

150

5	25
4	40
3	60
6	65

1500

10	25
30	40
50	60
20	65

800

4	150
10	195
12	75
5	60

1200

10	10
30	20
50	30
20	50

Explaining Multiplication

Explain how each student multiplied 29 by 8.

Chalkboard Talk

Find the product of 29 and 8.

$$29$$
$$\times\ 8$$
$$72\ (9 \times 8)$$
$$160\ (8 \times 20)$$
$$232\ (add)$$

$$30 \times 8 = 240$$
Subtract 1×8
That's $240 - 8 = 232$
So $29 \times 8 = 232$

Try these:

1.
$$62$$
$$\times\ 5$$

2.
$$230$$
$$\times\ 8$$

3. 326×4

4. 37×2

1. Interview people to find out when they need to multiply. Also find out when they need an exact answer and when they need an estimate.

2. These students think about how to multiply 58 by 6. Think about their procedures. Draw an explanation of how you multiply 58 by 6.

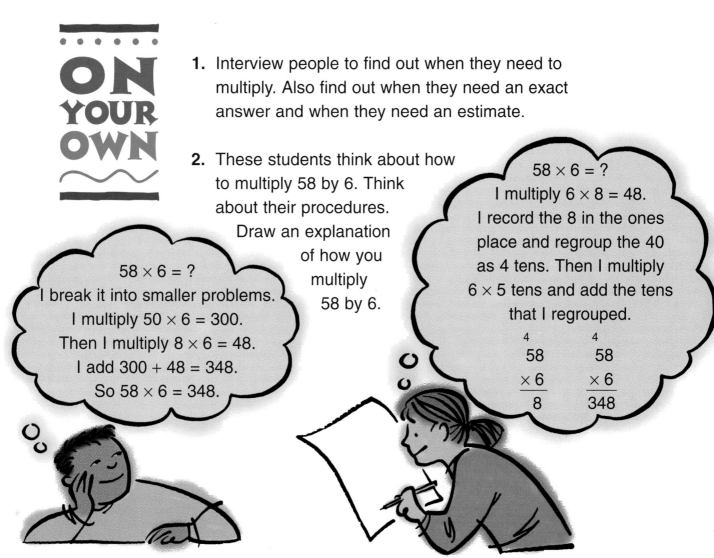

$58 \times 6 = ?$
I break it into smaller problems.
I multiply $50 \times 6 = 300$.
Then I multiply $8 \times 6 = 48$.
I add $300 + 48 = 348$.
So $58 \times 6 = 348$.

$58 \times 6 = ?$
I multiply $6 \times 8 = 48$.
I record the 8 in the ones place and regroup the 40 as 4 tens. Then I multiply 6×5 tens and add the tens that I regrouped.

$$\begin{array}{r} {}^{4} \\ 58 \\ \times\, 6 \\ \hline 8 \end{array} \qquad \begin{array}{r} {}^{4} \\ 58 \\ \times\, 6 \\ \hline 348 \end{array}$$

3. Write a note to convince someone that $326 \times 4 = 1304$.

4. *My Journal:* What questions do you have about multiplication?

Practise Your Skills

Find the products.

1. 32×8 2. 47×6 3. 93×5 4. 71×8

5. 384×6 6. 195×3 7. 704×8 8. 187×5

9. $\begin{array}{r} 58 \\ \times\, 4 \\ \hline \end{array}$ 10. $\begin{array}{r} 72 \\ \times\, 9 \\ \hline \end{array}$ 11. $\begin{array}{r} 386 \\ \times\, 2 \\ \hline \end{array}$ 12. $\begin{array}{r} 408 \\ \times\, 6 \\ \hline \end{array}$

DOUBLES or LATTICE work?

Have you ever wondered if other people developed procedures for multiplication different from yours?

The lattice method of multiplication is believed to have been used first in India. Chinese, Arabs, and Persians all favoured this method. The method found its way into Italian texts in the 14th century.

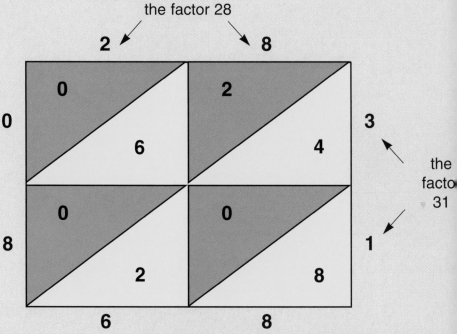

the factor 28

the factor 31

1. What is the product of 8 and 3? of 8 and 1? of 2 and 3? of 2 and 1? Find these products within the lattice.

2. Add diagonally. The first diagonal is the triangle in the lower right corner. The 8 in it means 8 ones.
The next diagonal has 4, 0, and 2. That makes 6 tens.
The next diagonal has 2, 6, and 0. That makes 8 hundreds.
The product is 868.

The doubles or duplication method of multiplication was used by the Egyptians. A version of this method is still used in Russia today.

$$1 \times 28 = 28$$
$$2 \times 28 = 56$$
$$4 \times 28 = 112$$
$$8 \times 28 = 224$$
$$16 \times 28 = 448$$
$$\overline{}$$
$$31 \times 28 = 868$$

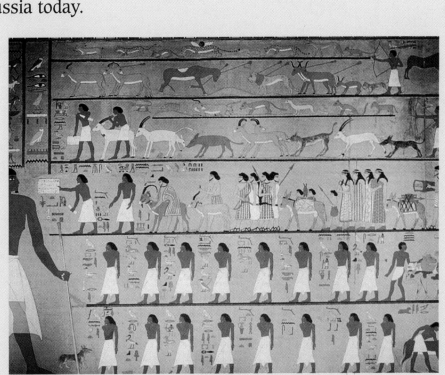

3 Use the duplication method. How would you find 7×28?

4 Find the product of 15 and 27 using duplication.

5 How do people you know multiply?

ARRAYS and *Remainders* GAME

Group
· ·

2 players

Materials
· ·

• Tiles

• Two number cubes labelled 1 to 6

• Recording sheets

Goal:

• To collect the most tiles

Game Rules:

. . . .

1 Roll two number cubes and use the numbers
rolled to make the least possible two-digit number.
Record the number and count that many tiles.

2 Each player rolls a number cube. The player who rolls the
greater number goes first.

3 The first player rolls one number cube and makes an array
of tiles with that number of rows.

> *For example, if there are 36 tiles to start and the player
> rolls 5, the array will have 5 rows with 7 tiles in each.
> There would be a remainder of one tile.*

The player records a division equation for the array.

> *For example, 36 ÷ 5 = 7 R1.*

The player keeps any remaining tile or tiles and passes
all the rest to the other player.

4 The next player takes a turn as described in step 3.

5 Repeat steps 1 to 4 for each round of the game until six
or fewer tiles are left in play.

▶ Use base ten blocks. Show what each complete array looks like. Write a division sentence that tells about each array.

1. 65 square units   **2.** 96 square units

8 columns

4 rows
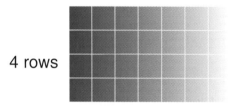
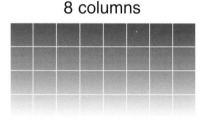

3. The Goodblankets are planning a rectangular patio with an area of 48 m². Find the possible lengths and widths they could use. Which would you suggest? Why?

4. *My Journal:* Suppose you roll a 1 in the Arrays and Remainders Game. Why won't you get a remainder?

Practise Your Skills

Solve.

1. 25 ÷ 5   **2.** 64 ÷ 8   **3.** 18 ÷ 9   **4.** 45 ÷ 5   **5.** 28 ÷ 7

6. 9⟌63   **7.** 4⟌32   **8.** 3⟌21   **9.** 9⟌36   **10.** 6⟌18

11. 22 ÷ 2   **12.** 84 ÷ 7   **13.** 75 ÷ 3   **14.** 72 ÷ 6   **15.** 92 ÷ 6

16. 8⟌96   **17.** 3⟌87   **18.** 8⟌76   **19.** 4⟌51   **20.** 7⟌74

Solving and Creating Problems

▶ Solve these problems with a partner. Use words and pictures so that others will understand your solutions.

1. A new bag of marbles costs 96¢. Suppose four friends share the cost. How much would each pay?

2. There are 60 marbles in the bag. How many marbles would each of the four friends get?

3. To win the marble game you need 24 points. Each time you hit a marble you get 3 points. How many times must you hit a marble to win?

4. Smaller packs of marbles cost 48¢.
   Gina has a nickel collection.
   How many nickels
   would she need to
   buy a package?

5. There are 30 small marbles
   and 18 larger marbles
   in a medium-sized package.
   How many of each would there be
   for four players?

6. Sparkle marbles cost 9¢ each. How many
   could you buy with 75¢?

7. Three friends are playing marbles. Rick has 20 marbles.
   Alex has 14 marbles. Connor has 7 marbles.
   a. Suppose the friends divide their marbles equally.
      How many will each person have?
   b. Suppose marbles cost 3¢ each. How much did
      each person pay for his marbles? How much
      did they pay altogether?

1. Make up a problem about marbles that someone could solve by dividing. Draw a picture to go with it.

2. What problem could be solved using the sentence $49 \div 4 = 12$ R1?

3. Is this correct? Explain how you decided.

$$\begin{array}{r} 21 \text{ R4} \\ 3\overline{)\,64} \end{array}$$

4. *My Journal:* How do you check division problems to see if they are correct?

Practise Your Skills

Use estimation. Tell whether each product is greater than or less than 500.

1. 58×7 **2.** 7×87 **3.** 5×115 **4.** 38×12

Use estimation. Tell whether each product is greater than or less than 1000.

5. 5×185 **6.** 4×265 **7.** 40×40 **8.** 198×6

List the numbers from 1 to 10 that will divide evenly into each number.

9. 30 **10.** 40 **11.** 50 **12.** 25

Explaining Division

Explain how each student divided 64 by 7.

Chalkboard Talk

How many sevens are there in sixty-four?

$64 \div 7 = ?$

7 14 21 28 35 42 49 56 63

There are 9 sevens in 64 and 1 left over.

$7)\overline{64}$

$7 \times 10 = 70$

So $7 \times 9 = 63$

$\begin{array}{r} 9\ R1 \\ 7)\overline{64} \end{array}$

Try these:

1. How many sevens are there in 50?

2. $75 \div 8$

3. $42 \div 5$

4. $4)\overline{27}$

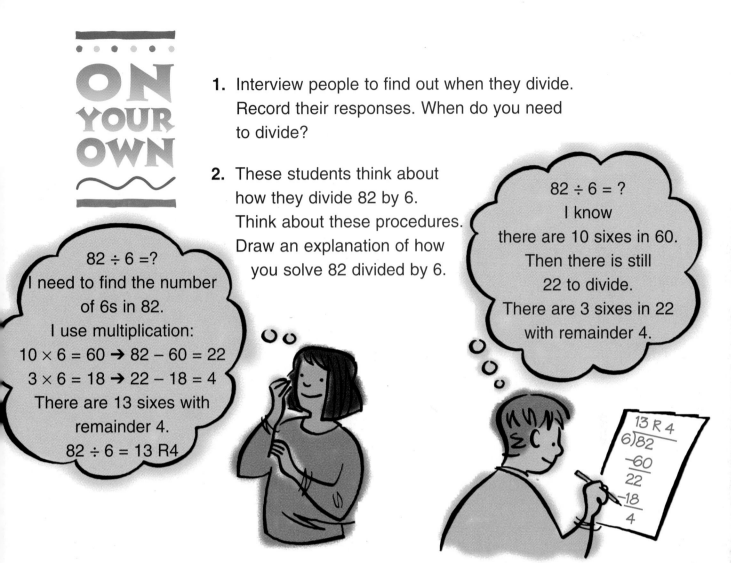

1. Interview people to find out when they divide. Record their responses. When do you need to divide?

2. These students think about how they divide 82 by 6. Think about these procedures. Draw an explanation of how you solve 82 divided by 6.

> 82 ÷ 6 =?
> I need to find the number of 6s in 82.
> I use multiplication:
> $10 \times 6 = 60 \rightarrow 82 - 60 = 22$
> $3 \times 6 = 18 \rightarrow 22 - 18 = 4$
> There are 13 sixes with remainder 4.
> $82 \div 6 = 13$ R4

> 82 ÷ 6 = ?
> I know there are 10 sixes in 60.
> Then there is still 22 to divide.
> There are 3 sixes in 22 with remainder 4.

3. Write a note to convince someone that $65 \div 3 = 21$ R2.

4. *My Journal:* How are multiplication and division related? How are division and subtraction related?

Practise Your Skills

1. How many eights are there in 57?

2. How many fours are there in 35?

3. $6 \overline{)88}$ 4. $9 \overline{)70}$ 5. $7 \overline{)81}$ 6. $3 \overline{)22}$ 7. $5 \overline{)98}$

8. $42 \div 6$ 9. $63 \div 3$ 10. $30 \div 4$ 11. $35 \div 2$ 12. $50 \div 6$

50 Years of Brushing Your Teeth

People around the world do many similar things. Choose an activity that you do every day and most likely will continue to do every day for the next 50 years. It may be brushing your teeth, or it may be something else.

- How many minutes will you spend?

- How many hours will you spend?

- How many days will you spend?

- How many weeks will you spend?

- How many months will you spend?

- How many years will you spend?

- How does your time compare with your classmates' times?

- How do you think this activity might differ in other parts of the world?

Equivalent Units of Time

1 minute = 60 seconds
1 day = 24 hours
1 week = 7 days
1 year = 365 days
1 year = 12 months
1 month = about 30 days

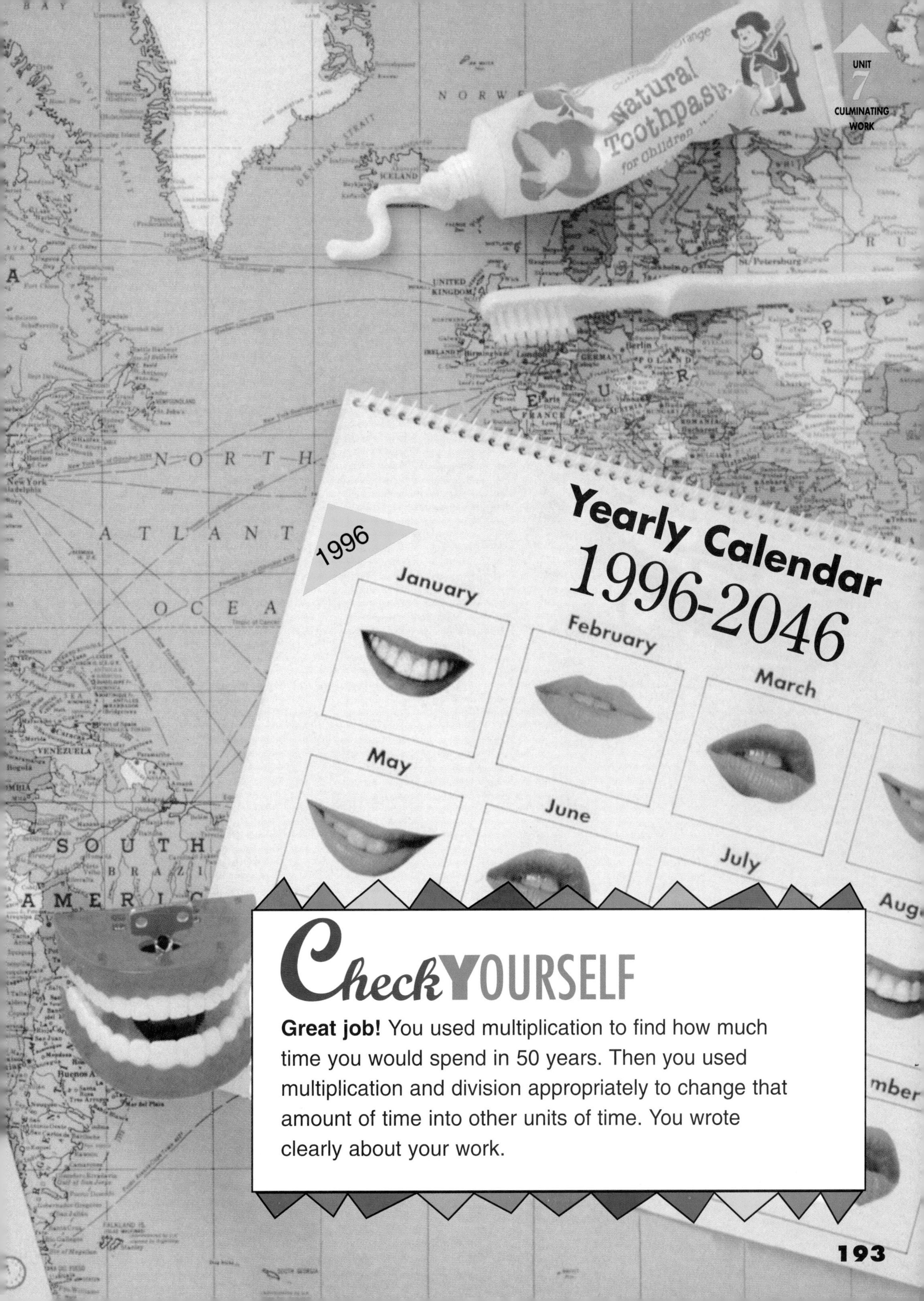

Yearly Calendar 1996-2046

1996

January
February
March
May
June
July
Aug

CheckYOURSELF

Great job! You used multiplication to find how much time you would spend in 50 years. Then you used multiplication and division appropriately to change that amount of time into other units of time. You wrote clearly about your work.

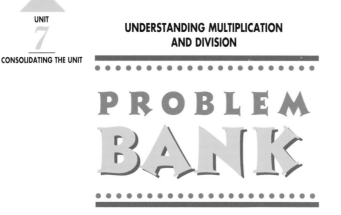
PROBLEM BANK

1. **a.** Write a multiplication sentence to show the number of squares in this array. How can you find the total?

31

6

b. Show two ways you could divide the array into two smaller arrays. Write a multiplication expression for each and show how to find the total.

2. Maria is planning to lay wall-to-wall carpet.
Each roll of carpet covers 32 m².
How many rolls of carpet does she need for a room 8 m × 12 m? Explain your answer.

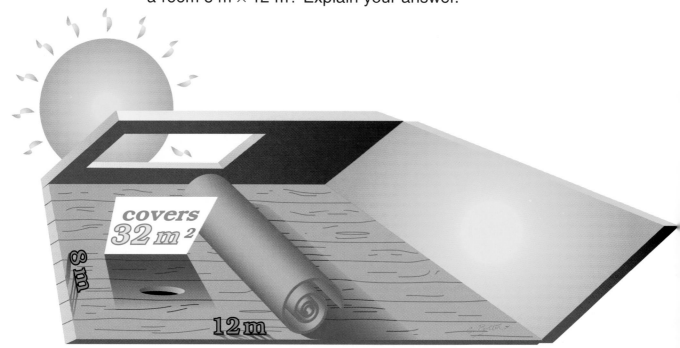

covers
32 m²

8 m

12 m

3. How much would it cost
for your family to see
a movie? Explain your
answer.

Ticket Prices

Adult	*$8.00*
Child	*$4.50*
Senior	*$6.00*

4. Estimate the number of glasses of milk you drink
in one month. Then estimate the number of glasses
you might drink in one year. Explain how you made
your estimates.

5. Record the number of hours you usually sleep each night.
How many hours do you sleep in one month? How many
hours do you sleep in one year? Show your work.

6. Keanan gets an allowance of $5.00 per week. Kyle gets
$22.00 per month. Who gets more allowance? How
did you decide?

7. Andrea's allowance is $240.00 per year. How much
does she receive per month? Explain your answer.

8. a. What do you think is a fair allowance per week?
b. How much is that for one month?
c. How much is that for one year?

9. Write a problem that could be solved using each sentence.
a. $93 \div 3 = 31$ **b.** $78 \times 6 = 468$

c. $6\overline{)75}$ with 12 R3 **d.** $415 \times 3 = 1245$

S K I L L BANK

FROM THIS UNIT

1. How many are in the array? Write a multiplication sentence to describe the total.

2. How many days old are you?

3. Multiply. Do only those questions with products greater than 200.
   a. 50×6　　**b.** 30×9　　**c.** 3×50　　**d.** 7×30

   e. 48×6　　**f.** 27×9　　**g.** 3×45　　**h.** 7×31

4. Divide. Do only those questions with remainders.
   a. $80 \div 6$　　**b.** $50 \div 9$　　**c.** $80 \div 5$　　**d.** $70 \div 3$

   e. $49 \div 4$　　**f.** $86 \div 2$　　**g.** $92 \div 7$　　**h.** $25 \div 8$

5. Make up a story problem that could be solved using each sentence.
   a. $24 \times 6 = 144$　　**b.** $98 \div 7 = 14$

6. Multiply.

a. 28	**b.** 16	**c.** 95	**d.** 461	**e.** 366
$\times 5$	$\times 4$	$\times 6$	$\times 7$	$\times 3$

f. 28	**g.** 28	**h.** 28	**i.** 28	**j.** 28
$\times 10$	$\times 100$	$\times 20$	$\times 50$	$\times 70$

7. Divide.
   a. $70 \div 3$　　**b.** $97 \div 8$　　**c.** $165 \div 5$　　**d.** $450 \div 6$

   e. $7 \overline{)\,84}$　　**f.** $4 \overline{)\,30}$　　**g.** $5 \overline{)\,54}$　　**h.** $2 \overline{)\,98}$

SKILL BANK
LOOKING BACK

1. Find the perimeter and area of each figure.

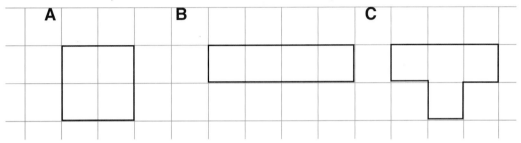

2. Find the area of each figure.

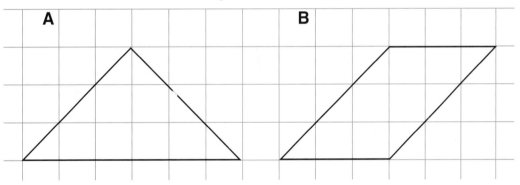

3. Write a fraction for each coloured part. Circle the fraction in each pair that is greater.

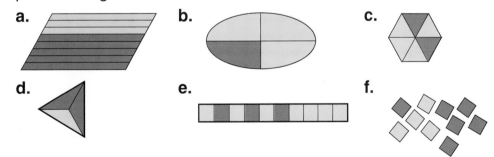

4. Which is greater, $\frac{3}{5}$ or 0.75?

5. Write each decimal as a fraction.

   a. 0.88   **b.** 0.80   **c.** 0.08   **d.** 0.8

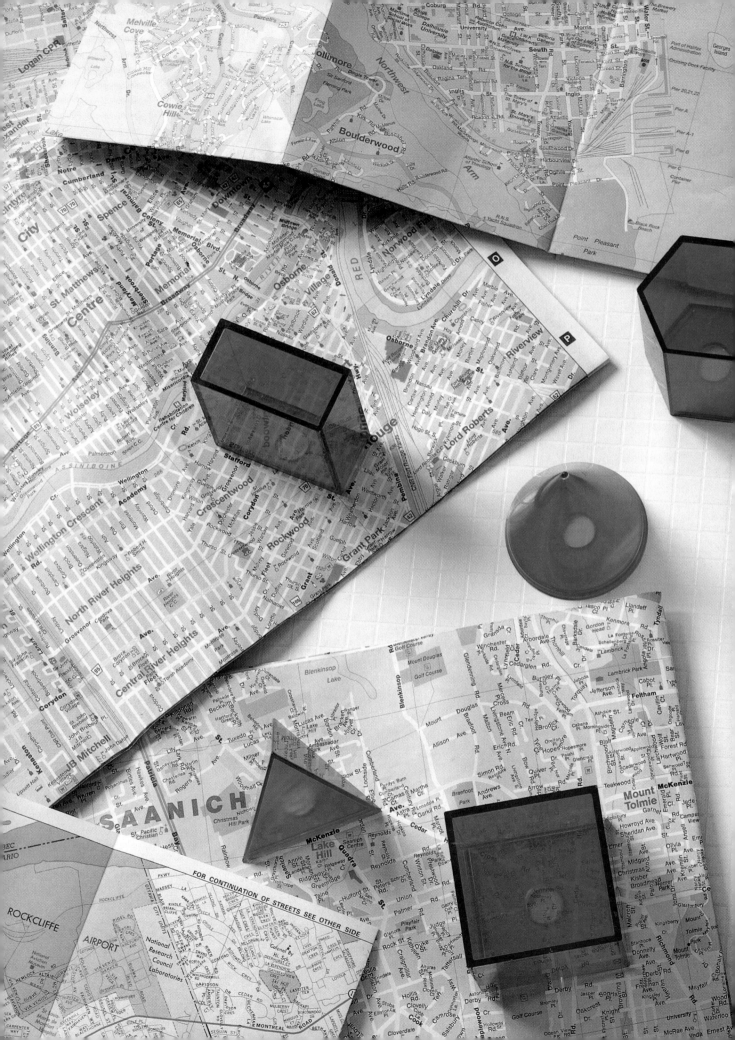

Placing Figures and Solids in Space

*H*ow can we describe figures and locations?

PLACING FIGURES AND
SOLIDS IN SPACE

S·T·A·R·T·I·N·G
OUT

1
- What figures do you see in this picture?
- What helps you to know the shapes of the buildings?
- How would you describe the locations of the streets to someone who couldn't see this picture?
- Why do you think many towns are laid out like this one?

My Journal: Imagine your own neighbourhood. What do you think it would look like from this view?

 **dentifying Lines**

These are horizontal lines.

These are not horizontal lines.

These are vertical lines.

These are not vertical lines.

These are parallel lines.

These are not parallel lines.

These are intersecting lines.

These are not intersecting lines.

These are perpendicular lines.

These are not perpendicular lines.

• What types of lines do you see?

Line	Definition	Examples in pictures	Examples in classroom
Parallel			
Horizontal			
Vertical			
Perpendicular			

You have already found many types of lines.
On this page you can find examples of lines of symmetry.

Find the lines of symmetry for these drawings.
Are they horizontal or vertical?

 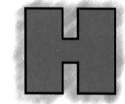 

  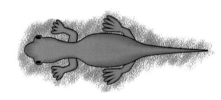

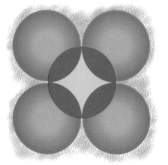

Words to Know

A **line of symmetry** separates a design or figure into parts that have the same size and shape.

1. Draw a design using at least five lines.
Don't let your partner see it. Tell your partner
how to draw the same design. Check to see how
closely the designs match. What words did you use
to describe the lines? What other words might
have been useful?

2. Look at the design on the geoboard.
    a. Name each of the coloured lines.
    b. Sketch the figure in your notebook.
       Draw the line of symmetry.
       What type of line is it?

3. Sit in a room at home. Find at least
one example for each type of line
shown on Student Book page 202.
Write about what you found.

4. *My Journal:* What makes parallel lines different
from other lines?

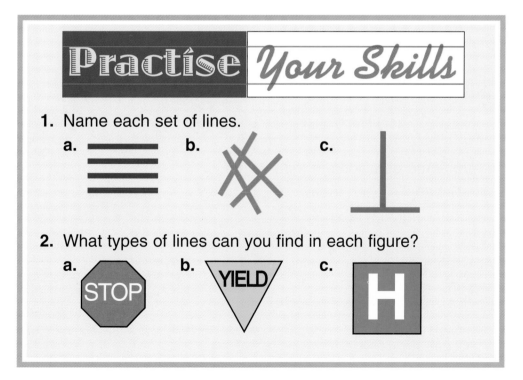

Practise Your Skills

1. Name each set of lines.
    a.   b.   c.

2. What types of lines can you find in each figure?
    a. STOP   b. YIELD   c. H

UNIT

8

ACTIVITY

2

Making Nets and Solids

► Examine the models you made to find out more about them.

Pyramids and prisms come in many shapes and sizes.
They are named by the shapes of the bases.

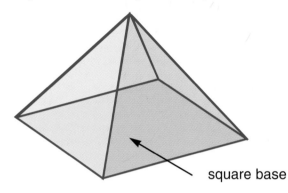

square base

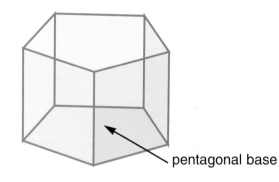

pentagonal base

This is a square-based pyramid.   This is a pentagonal prism.

1. What are the names of your models?

2. How are prisms and pyramids alike? How are they different?
   Make a chart to describe them.

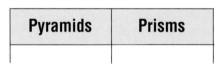

Pyramids	Prisms

Here are some questions to think about.
• What shape is each face?
• Are there parallel faces?
• Is there a face that is parallel to the base?
• Are some edges perpendicular?

▶ What type of solid do you think this net will make?

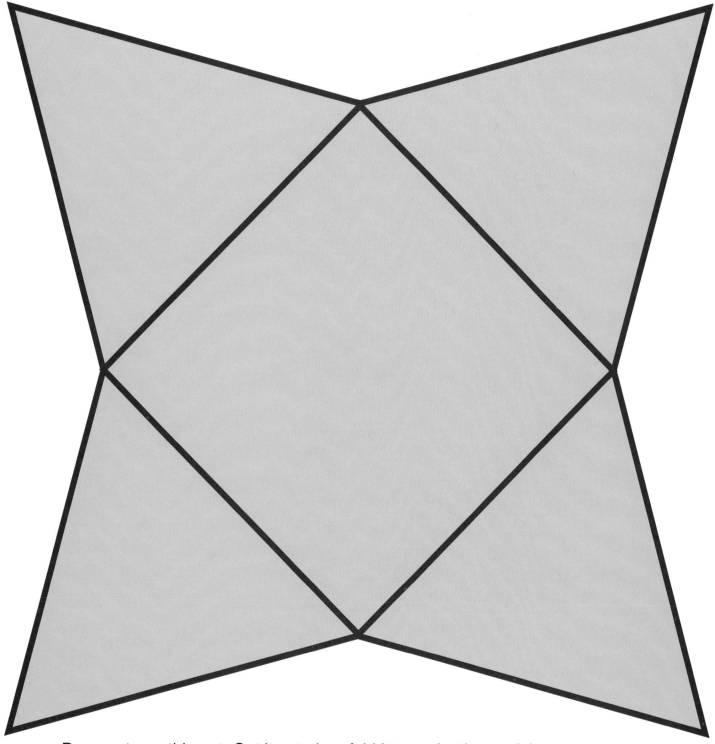

Draw or trace this net. Cut it out, then fold it to make the model.

▶ What do you know now?

1. Which nets were folded
to make each model?
Write to tell how you know.

a.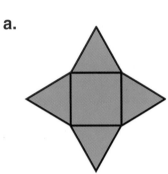

b.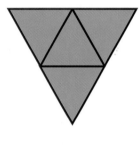

c.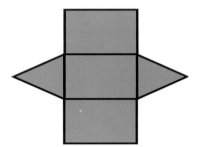

d.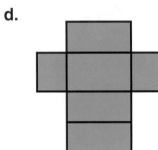

e.

f.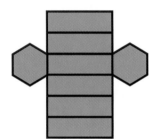

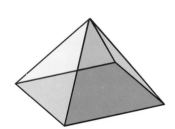
square-based pyramid

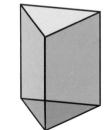
triangular prism

pentagonal pyramid

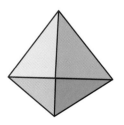
triangular pyramid

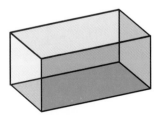
rectangular prism

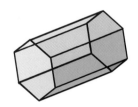
hexagonal prism

2. What colour is the face that will be parallel to the red face when the net is folded?

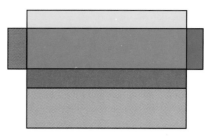

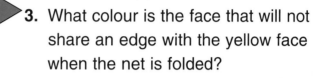

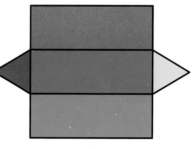

3. What colour is the face that will not share an edge with the yellow face when the net is folded?

4. What colours are the faces that will be parallel when the net is folded?

5. *My Journal:* What do you know about pyramids and prisms that you didn't know before?

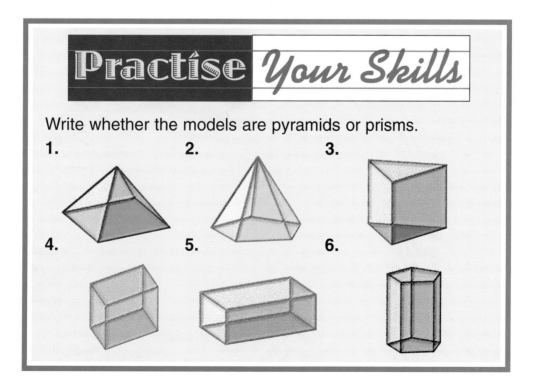

Practise Your Skills

Write whether the models are pyramids or prisms.

1.

2.

3.

4.

5.

6.

209

EARLY
SKYSCRAPERS

Have you ever wondered what figures other people used in their architecture? The Egyptians built pyramids like the Chephren Pyramid. You can see that triangles were used. The pyramids of Egypt were huge structures that could reach 146 m in height. The Mayans and Aztecs in Mexico and Central America also built structures sometimes called the Pyramids of the New World. The Pyramid of the Sun in Mexico is a step pyramid that is 66 m high. The Temple of the Warriors at Chichen Itza is another famous pyramid.

Chephren Pyramid

Temple of the Warriors

The Muttart Gallery

1 What modern buildings have you seen or seen pictures of that are shaped like pyramids?

2 Describe the faces of the Chephren Pyramid. What shape do you think the bottom is?

3 How do the faces of the Mexican pyramids differ from triangular faces?

4 Construct a pyramid from paper. First decide how many faces you will need and what their shapes should be.

211

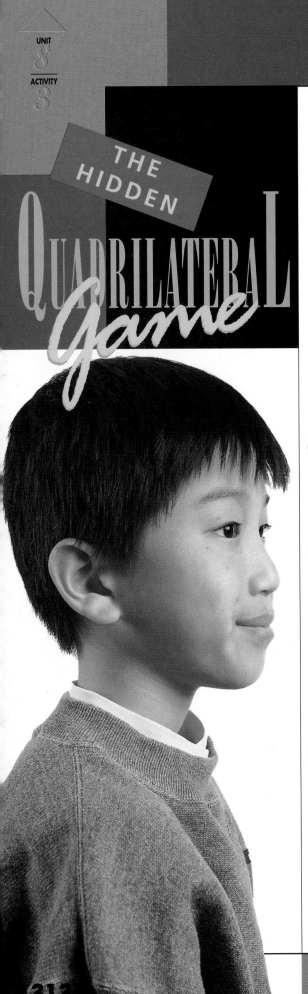

THE HIDDEN QUADRILATERAL Game

Group

2 players

Materials

Each player needs:

• Quadrilaterals, Activity Master 28
• Two copies of 2-cm Grid Paper, Activity Master 17

Game Rules

1 Label the grids as shown. One grid is your recording sheet; the other is for hiding a quadrilateral.

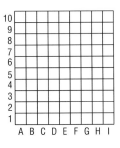

2 Set up a barrier so that you can't see your partner's grids. Now secretly choose a quadrilateral and place it on one of your grids.

3 Take turns guessing the location of each other's hidden quadrilateral. Use the letter-number pairs to ask whether part of the quadrilateral is in that space on the grid.

4 Record on your grid what you find out with each question.

5 On any of your turns you can ask one Yes-No question about your partner's hidden quadrilateral. For example: **Are all sides equal?** or **Are both pairs of sides parallel?**

6 The first player to identify the hidden quadrilateral and its location wins.

21

Using Maps

▶ What features does a map have?

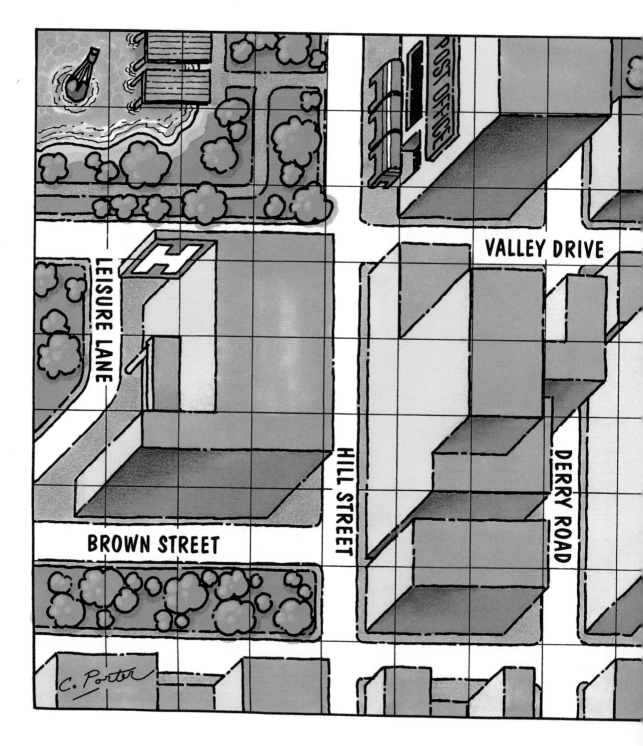

LEISURE LANE

VALLEY DRIVE

POST OFFICE

HILL STREET

DERRY ROAD

BROWN STREET

C. Porter

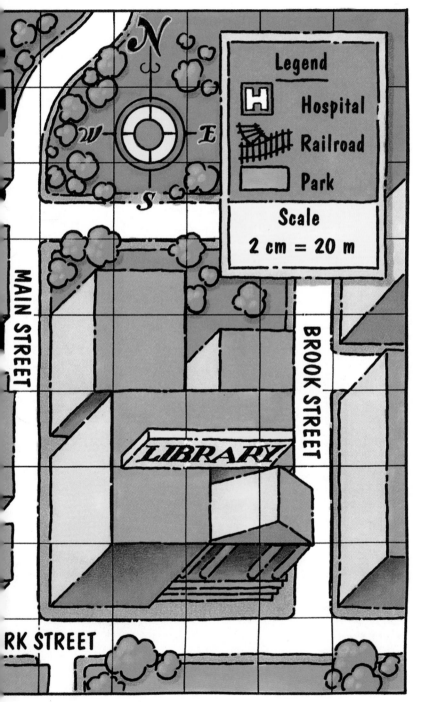

1. Which streets run parallel to Main Street?
2. Which streets intersect at the library?
3. a. Describe a route that would take you from the library to the post office?
   b. Describe another route.
4. In what direction would you be travelling from the hospital to the library? from the library to the hospital?
5. About how far is a route from the library's front door to the intersection of Brown Street and Hill Street?
6. Which is farther, from Park Street to Valley Drive or from Leisure Lane to Main Street?
7. Which streets are perpendicular to each other?

▶ Use this map for Problems 1 and 2.

1. Pick two locations. Describe a route
from one place to the other. Describe a different
route to take you back to where you started.

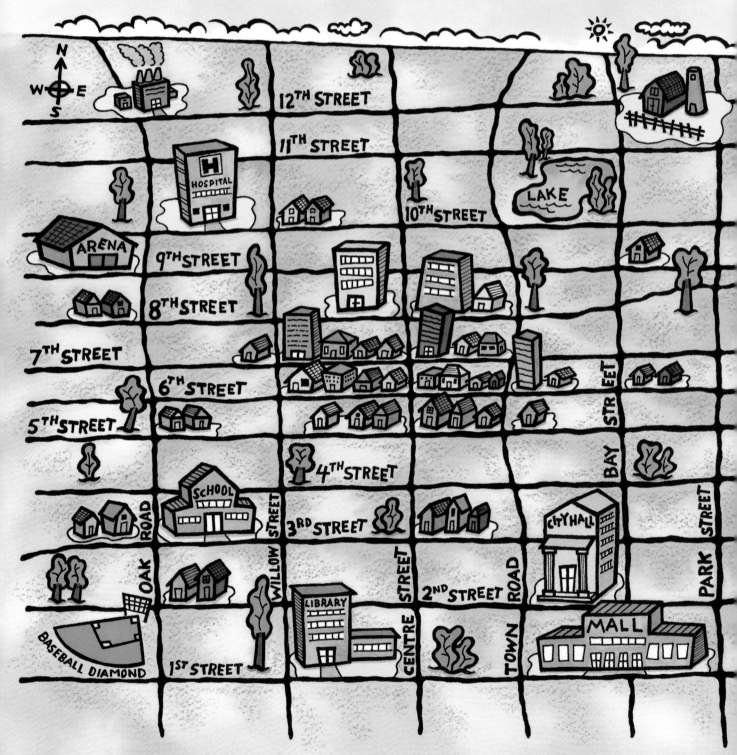

2. Find the section where most people live. How could you describe the location of this section of town?

3. Describe a route you could take from your classroom to the school office.

4. Describe the route you take from home to school.

5. *My Journal:* What do you think makes a map easy to read?

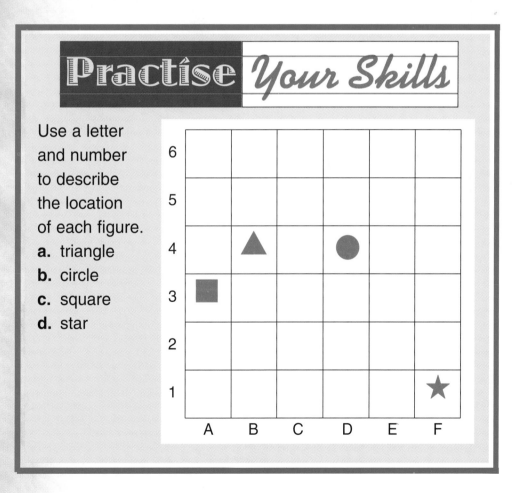

Practíse Your Skills

Use a letter and number to describe the location of each figure.
a. triangle
b. circle
c. square
d. star

CALLING TOWN PLANNERS

Your job is to plan a new town.

- As a class, decide on some buildings and locations to include in the town.

- Talk with your group about other places you would like to include.

- Make a map to show where the buildings and places would be located.
  Make sure that your map includes a legend, a scale, and a grid.

- Choose one building from your town and make a model of it.

- Write a description of your model and why you chose it.

2 cm = 100 m

Check YOURSELF

Great job! You have worked together to make a map that has all the places and buildings that it should. You have a legend and a scale that are easy to understand. Your model of a town building is complete and you have described it clearly.

O P

Y Z

PROBLEM BANK

1. Draw a picture that includes a pair of horizontal parallel lines and a pair of vertical parallel lines. Try not to make them obvious. Ask a friend to try to find both sets of lines.

2. Use what you know about different types of lines to write a description of this stained glass. Include enough information so that someone could draw it from your description.

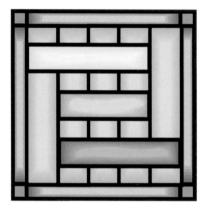

3. Look through a magazine to find pictures with symmetry. Are the lines of symmetry horizontal or vertical? Write a label for each picture.

4. Here is a model made using two nets. Sketch what you think each net looked like. Write a description of each net.

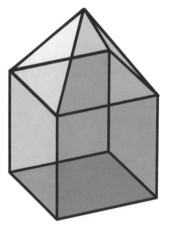

5. a. Describe two paths for travelling from point X to point Y.

   b. Where would you put point Z so that it is as far from point X as it is from point Y?

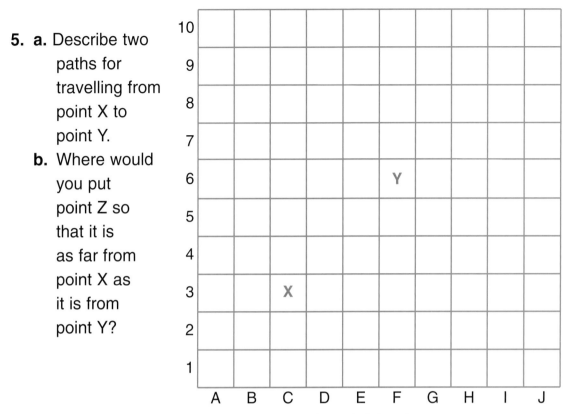

6. Use the grid to describe the location of each island.

7. Use the grid to estimate each distance.

   a. the length from east to west of Grey Island

   b. the width from north to south of Blue Island

   c. the distance north from the top of Red Island to the top of Blue Island

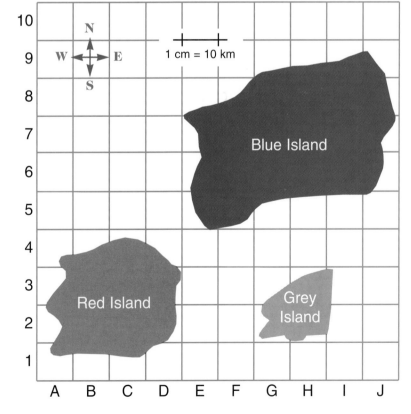

1. Use the terms parallel, intersecting, horizontal, vertical, or perpendicular to describe these lines.

a.   b.   c.

2. I have five flat faces. One of my faces is square. My other faces are the same shape. What solid am I?

3. Which of these letters are made with perpendicular line segments?

E   S   W   A   B   O   D   F   H

4. Which of these nets can be used to make a hexagonal prism?

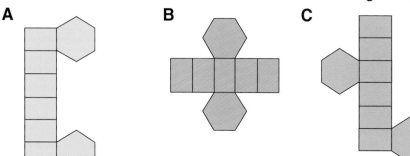

A   B   C

5. Copy and complete this picture so that it is symmetrical.

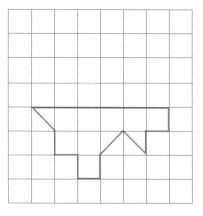

6. Describe a route for getting from your classroom to the office.

222

S K I L L
BANK
LOOKING BACK

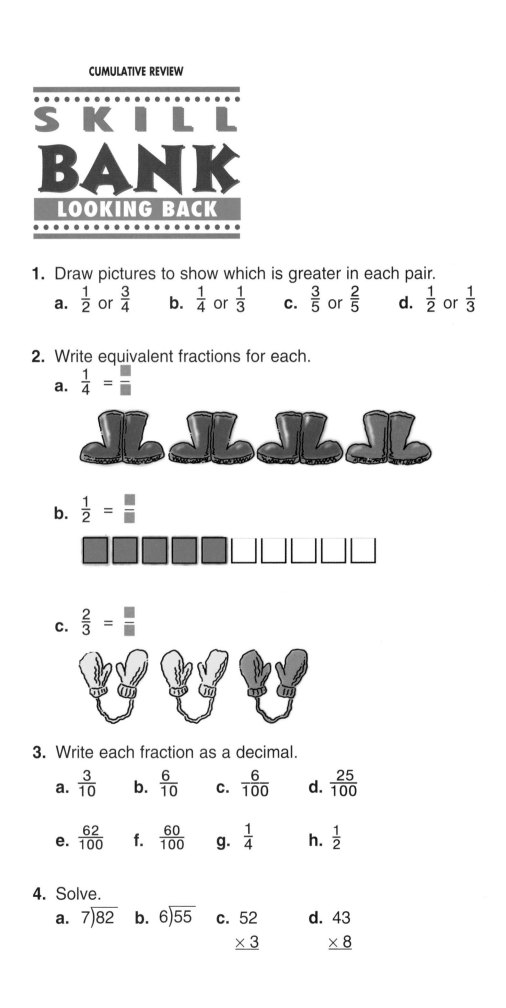

1. Draw pictures to show which is greater in each pair.
   a. $\frac{1}{2}$ or $\frac{3}{4}$ **b.** $\frac{1}{4}$ or $\frac{1}{3}$ **c.** $\frac{3}{5}$ or $\frac{2}{5}$ **d.** $\frac{1}{2}$ or $\frac{1}{3}$

2. Write equivalent fractions for each.
   a. $\frac{1}{4} = \frac{\blacksquare}{\blacksquare}$

   b. $\frac{1}{2} = \frac{\blacksquare}{\blacksquare}$

   c. $\frac{2}{3} = \frac{\blacksquare}{\blacksquare}$

3. Write each fraction as a decimal.
   a. $\frac{3}{10}$ **b.** $\frac{6}{10}$ **c.** $\frac{6}{100}$ **d.** $\frac{25}{100}$

   e. $\frac{62}{100}$ **f.** $\frac{60}{100}$ **g.** $\frac{1}{4}$ **h.** $\frac{1}{2}$

4. Solve.
   a. $7\overline{)82}$ **b.** $6\overline{)55}$ **c.** $52 \atop \underline{\times 3}$ **d.** $43 \atop \underline{\times 8}$

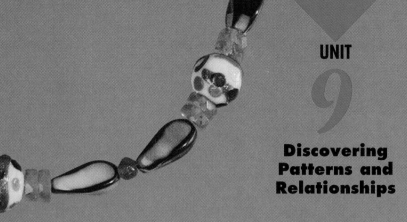

UNIT

9

Discovering Patterns and Relationships

*H*ow can we use patterns to predict?

225

DISCOVERING PATTERNS
AND RELATIONSHIPS

S·T·A·R·T·I·N·G
S OUT

1 • What patterns do you see in the garden pictured here?

• What other patterns do you see in this garden? Describe them.

• If you wanted to make the flower bed twice as long, how would you plant the shrubs and flowers to continue the pattern?

• Write a problem that a friend could solve about a pattern on this page.

My Journal: Tell about some times when you have used patterns.

Describing Patterns

Use models and complete the T-tables to answer the questions.

1. How many pieces do you need to build a castle wall with 6 towers?

Number of Towers	Number of Pieces
1	3
2	8
3	13
4	?
5	?
6	?

2. How many pieces do you need to build a 5-tower wall?

Number of Towers	Number of Pieces
1	2
2	5
3	8
4	?
5	?
6	?

3. How many towers are in a 36-piece wall?

Number of Towers	Number of Pieces
1	4
2	12
3	20
4	?
5	?
6	?

ON YOUR OWN

1. How many Power Polygon pieces does it take to make a row with 10 green triangles?

Triangles	Power Polygons
1	3
2	5
3	7
4	?

2. Make up a pattern using clapping. Begin your pattern. Ask a family member to clap to continue your pattern. Try another one. Then switch roles. Describe your pattern in words and make a T-table for it.

3. *My Journal:* Do you enjoy making and recording patterns? Explain.

CLAPS

long	short
2	3
4	6
6	?

Practise Your Skills

1. Show the next three terms in each pattern.

   a. 4, 7, 10, …
   b. 13, 24, 35, …
   c. 99, 87, 75, …

   d.

2. a. Complete the T-table.
   b. How much would be earned in 10 hours? 15 hours?

Number of Hours	Money Earned
1	$ 6.00
2	$ 12.00
3	$ 18.00
4	?
5	?
6	?

NOTES ON
Computers

Dr. Donna Auguste

Have you ever wondered how patterns are used in music? Or in computers? Both African-Canadians and First Nations People have long musical traditions that use interesting and complex rhythmic patterns, but many have never been written down. With new technological developments, computers can be used to write some of these musical patterns.

Dr. Donna Auguste, shown at left, led the team who designed a hand-held, pen-based computer that recognizes handwriting patterns and converts them to typed text. She is also a musician interested in translating African-American, African-Canadian, and First Nations musical patterns to written notes. Dr. Auguste turns song into writing when she creates arrangements with her computer for her gospel choir.

Choir of gospel singers

- **1** Look in a music text or at a piece of sheet music. What patterns do you see? What systems are used to show how high or low a note is? How long or short its duration is?

- **2** Listen to music of different types and from different cultures. What patterns do you hear? How would you show or explain those patterns to someone?

- **3** Play a piece of your favourite music on a recorder or other classroom instrument. What patterns can your classmates hear?

231

Using T-Tables

Use models and complete the T-tables to answer the questions.

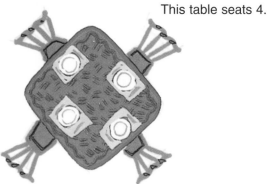

This table seats 4.

These tables together seat 6.

How many people can be seated when 8 tables are placed in a row?

Number of Tables	Number of People Seated
1	4
2	6
3	8
4	?

How many toothpicks are needed for 4 triangles? for 6 triangles?

Number of Triangles	Number of Toothpicks
1	3
2	5
3	7
4	?
5	?
6	?

With 3 toothpicks you can make 1 triangle. You need 5 to make 2 triangles.

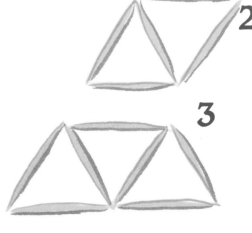

1

2

3

1. Suppose you need to seat 22 people at square tables placed end-to-end to make one big table. Each table seats 1 person on a side. How many tables do you need? Explain your plan.

2. Suppose you had 17 toothpicks to continue the triangle design on page 232. Your design left off at 6 triangles. How many triangles can you build? Explain your thinking.

3. *My Journal:* Did you prefer the table or the toothpick problem? Explain.

Practíse Your Skills

A farmer used 12 sections of fence to enclose 4 fields. More fields can be added in the same pattern.

1. How many sections of fence will the farmer need to enclose ten fields?

2. What pattern do you notice in the number of sections?

Number of Fields	Number of Sections
4	12
5	15
6	17
7	?
8	?
9	?
10	?

CHAIN PATTERNS

How does the perimeter change as the chain gets longer?

Number of Triangles	Perimeter
1	3
2	4
3	5
4	?
5	?
6	?
7	?
8	?
9	?
10	?

Now choose two figures other than a triangle to investigate. How does the perimeter change as a chain of figures gets longer? Here are some things to think about.

• Do you think the patterns will be the same as for triangles? Why or why not?

• How can a T-table help you predict what will happen?

• How many rows will the T-table need before you can make a good prediction?

CheckYOURSELF

Great job! You created a polygon chain pattern. Your T-table accurately showed what happened as the chain of figures got longer. You used the T-table to make and test some predictions about how the perimeter changes. You identified the patterns and were sure they would work for any number of figures. You wrote to describe clearly the patterns.

235

P R O B L E M
BANK

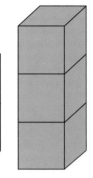

1. Here are stacks of cubes. Think about how many square faces you can see if you look at all the sides and the top of a stack.

   a. How many square faces can you see on 10 stacked cubes? Complete the T-table to find out.

   b. Write to describe patterns you see in the completed T- table.

Number of Cubes	Number of Square Faces
1	5
2	9
3	13
.	?
.	?
.	?
10	?

2. Here is a growing pattern of squares. Complete the T-table.

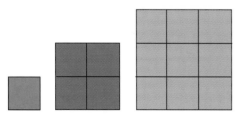

Figure	Small Squares
1	1
2	4
3	9
4	?
5	?
6	?

3. Write to describe patterns you see in the completed T-table in problem 2.

REVIEWING THE UNIT

1. **a.** Describe the patterns in the nine times table.
   (Look at the digits in the ones column. Then look
   at the digits in the tens column.)
   0, 9, 18, 27, 36, 45, …

   b. Predict the products: 11 x 9, 12 x 9.

2. How many Power Polygon pieces would
   it take to make a design with ten green
   triangles if this pattern continues?
   Use a T-table.

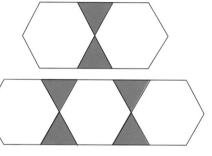

CUMULATIVE REVIEW

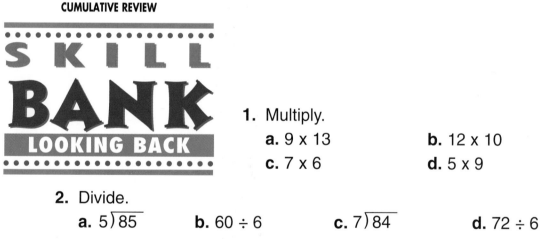

1. Multiply.

   a. 9 x 13   **b.** 12 x 10

   c. 7 x 6   **d.** 5 x 9

2. Divide.

   a. $5\overline{)85}$ **b.** 60 ÷ 6   **c.** $7\overline{)84}$ **d.** 72 ÷ 6

3. The swift is a bird that flies very fast. One swift flew at a top
   speed of 192 km/h. Suppose this bird flew in a straight line,
   at its top speed, for 5 hours. How far would it travel?

4. Name a solid for each set of faces.

   a. 6 squares   **b.** 2 triangles and 3 rectangles

   c. 2 squares and   **d.** 1 square and 4 equilateral
       4 rectangles   triangles

237

10

**Exploring
Outcomes**

What are
the
chances?

1 • Describe each of these pictures using any of these words: likely, certain, possible, unlikely, uncertain, impossible.

• Write about a situation you could add to this page. What words would you use to describe it?

My Journal: What are you likely to do today?
What are you unlikely to do today?

2 • Which booth would you choose to try? Why?

• At which booth do you think you have a very good chance of winning? Explain your thinking.

• At which booth is it equally likely that you will win or lose? Explain your thinking.

• At which booth is it unlikely that you will win? Explain your thinking.

My Journal: What does the word "chance" mean to you?

SORRY

PRIZE

PRIZE AGAIN

SPIN AGAIN

PRIZE

SPIN FOR A PRIZE

25¢ a Try

GET A RED GUMBALL WIN A LARGE BEAR

GET A GREEN GUMBALL WIN A SMALL BEAR

Outcomes That Are Not Equally Likely

How many times out of 100 spins might the pointer land on orange? Why?

Follow these directions:

1 Use the Spinner Circle and a paper clip to make a spinner with two colours so that you might expect to get one of the colours 70 out of 100 spins.

2 Write to tell why you think your spinner will give 70 out of 100 of one colour.

3 Do 100 trials with your spinner. Record your findings. Did you get 70 out of 100 of one colour?

4 Would you like to try again? If so, use the results from your first spinner to help you design another spinner.

1. In 100 spins of this spinner, how many times do you predict the pointer will land on orange? How many times will you spin gold? Explain your thinking. If the same spinner were spun 500 times, how many of each colour do you predict you would get? Explain.

For problems 2, 3, and 4 write the number of times you predict each colour will come up in 1000 spins. Tell how you predicted.

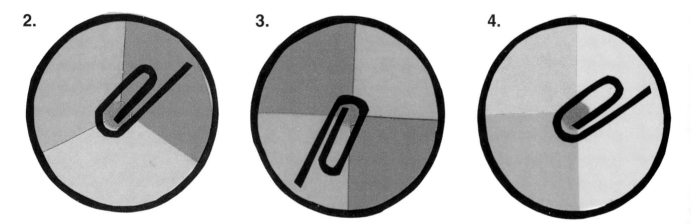

2.

3.

4.

5. *My Journal:* What did you learn that was new?

Practise Your Skills

Draw a spinner that you think will give the results shown.

1. 55 orange
   45 green
   in 100 spins

2. 200 blue
   300 orange
   in 500 spins

3. 600 gold
   300 blue
   100 red
   in 1000 spins

Estimating Chances

Materials
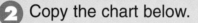

1 clear plastic cup
1 rubber band
1 sheet of plastic wrap
10 small folded pieces of construction paper

1 Place the folded papers in the cup. Cover the cup with the plastic and secure using the rubber band.

2 Copy the chart below.

Possible Outcome	My Prediction	Tally	Actual Outcome
fold down			
fold up			

3 Predict the number of times each outcome will occur in 100 trials (taken 10 at a time). Record your predictions in the chart.

4 Shake the cup, remove the wrap, and toss the papers on your desk.

5 Mark a tally for each of the 10 folded papers with the appropriate outcome.

6 Repeat the experiment 9 more times for a total of 100 outcomes.

ON YOUR OWN

Conduct 50 trials of each experiment below. For each experiment, make a chart like the one on page 246. Then write a sentence to describe the chance of each outcome occurring.

1. Toss a bottle cap or shaving cream can cap.

2. Label the sides of a flat eraser 1 and 2 and toss it.

3. *My Journal:* Explain what you know about equally likely and not equally likely outcomes.

Practise *Your Skills*

Describe the chances of rolling each outcome with a cube numbered 1 to 6.

1. 6

2. 1 or more

3. 3 or more

RACING SQUARES

Group

2 players

Materials

Each group needs:

- 2 number cubes

- 39 centimetre squares cut from the bottom of a sheet of grid paper or centimetre cubes

- a 7 by 11 grid like this drawn on the rest of the grid paper

2	3	4	5	6	7	8	9	10	11	12

Game Rules:

1 Roll two number cubes.

2 Add the numbers that come up to get a sum.

3 Place a centimetre square or cube above that sum on the grid paper race horse chart.

4 Keep going until one column of centimetre squares reaches the finish line. That number is the winner!

FINISH LINE

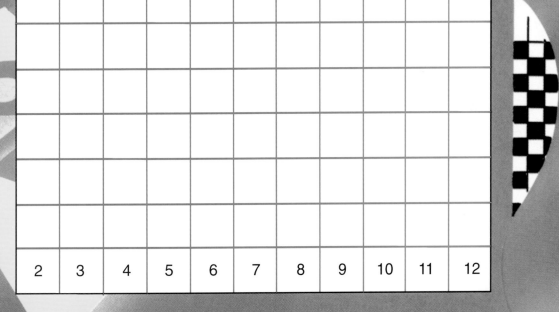

2	3	4	5	6	7	8	9	10	11	12

Each set of information below shows
the results of an experiment. Study the information.
Then copy the spinner or number cube. Colour the
spinner or write numbers on the cube to show what it
might have looked like. Explain your reasoning.

1. 50 spins of a spinner

outcome	times spun
yellow	40
green	10

2. 100 spins of a spinner

outcome	times spun
blue	38
red	31
green	31

3. 100 rolls of a number cube

outcome	times rolled
1	54
2	31
3	15

4. 500 rolls of a number cube

outcome	times rolled
1	80
3	350
5	70

5. *My Journal:* What have you learned about probable outcomes? Explain.

Practise Your Skills

1. A bag contains 5 marbles. One marble was picked, then returned. This was done 200 times. Here are the results.

outcome	times picked
red	80
blue	120

Draw the 5 marbles. Colour them to show how many of each colour.

2. A bag contains 6 marbles. One marble was picked, then returned. This was done 300 times. Here are the results.

outcome	times picked
black	203
red	47
green	50

Draw the 6 marbles. Colour them to show how many of each colour.

SKILL OR LUCK?

Have you ever wondered what kinds of games of chance people play? Many different hand games are played by First Nations peoples. In one game, two teams of 4 players sit opposite each other. Each player hides a small black reed in one hand and a small white reed in the other. The first player on one team guesses in which hand the first player of the other team holds the white reed. If the guess is correct, the guessing team gets 3 tokens. Then the other team has a turn to guess. The first team to get 15 tokens wins.

In another game a wooden ball, 2.5 cm in diameter, or a pebble is dropped by an extended arm at shoulder height into a shell 7.5 cm in diameter. The goal is to drop the object into the shell so that it goes inside and remains inside. Each player has 3 turns.

1 Which game is based only on luck?

2 Which game requires some skill?

Finding Chances of Two Events

Large grab bag

Small grab bag

Raimundo

Wish List

Panda
yoyo

You pull a pair of jeans and a
T-shirt out of your closet to wear.
You have four colours of jeans:
black, blue, red, and tan.
You have four colours of
T-shirts: black, white,
blue, and green.

1. How many jeans and T-shirt
   combinations are possible?

Use words like certain, very likely, unlikely,
and impossible to describe how likely
you think it is that you will choose each
of the following to wear.

2. a pair of tan jeans

3. a pair of blue jeans
   and a white T-shirt

4. a pair of green jeans
   and a grey T-shirt

5. a pair of jeans

6. *My Journal:* What have you
   learned about solving combination
   problems? Explain.

All Possible Combinations

For each of experiments 1 to 4:

a. Predict how likely the event is.

b. List all possible outcomes for the experiment.

c. Evaluate your prediction. How likely do you think the event is?

d. Draw a line like the one below. Mark it to show your new prediction.

e. Write to describe your findings.

```
0                                                              1
├──────────┼──────────────┼──────────────┼──────────┤
impossible    very           about           very       certain
              unlikely       even            likely
```

Experiment 1: Toss a coin and spin the spinner at the right.
Event: heads and green

Experiment 2: Roll a number cube (1– 6) and spin the spinner at the left.
Event: even number and an A or a B

Experiment 3: Choose two names from the bag, replace them, and draw again.
Event: Albert and Rita

ALBERT KECIA SAN CHUNG RITA

Experiment 4: Toss three different coins.
Event: three heads

1. You and a friend each secretly choose one of the number cards below. How likely is it that you each choose the same number? If you each choose a number less than 30, how likely is it that you choose the same number?

| 43 | 52 | 38 | 27 | 66 | 71 |

2. Redraw the three spinners so that the chance of each spinner landing on yellow is very likely.

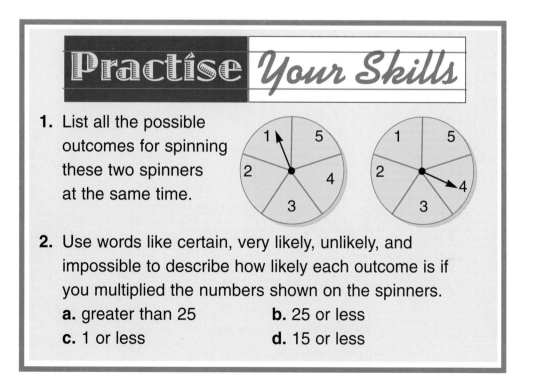

3. *My Journal:* What have you learned about finding outcomes for combinations of two events?

Practise Your Skills

1. List all the possible outcomes for spinning these two spinners at the same time.

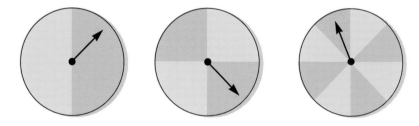

2. Use words like certain, very likely, unlikely, and impossible to describe how likely each outcome is if you multiplied the numbers shown on the spinners.
   a. greater than 25   b. 25 or less
   c. 1 or less   d. 15 or less

WHAT ARE YOUR CHANCES?

Each box of a certain kind of cereal contains one of four different prizes. How many boxes of cereal would you need to buy to get all four prizes?

One way of finding out is to use a spinner to do a simulation. Make a spinner like the one on the next page and use it to do a simulation of the prize problem.

Create a simulation to try to get all four prizes. Make a prediction before you start. Use your simulation to test your prediction.

CheckYOURSELF

Great job! You created a simulation that matches the conditions of the prize problem. You used the simulation to help explain how many boxes you would need to buy to get four different prizes.

1. If you were to spin this spinner 100 times, how many greens do you predict you will get? How many blues? Explain your thinking. If you were to spin this same spinner 1000 times, how many of each colour do you predict you would get? Explain your thinking.

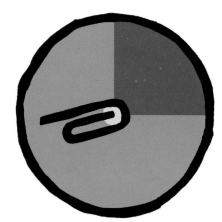

2. Write the number of times you predict each colour will come up in 1000 spins of these spinners:

  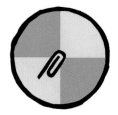

3. Draw spinners that you think will give each group of results shown:
   a. 35 orange, 65 blue in 100 spins
   b. 100 red, 400 green in 500 spins
   c. 300 blue, 500 green, 200 red in 1000 spins

4. Create a problem about a likely or unlikely chance of something happening. Test your problem and write it out. Pass it to a friend and have that friend solve your problem. Were the results what you expected? Explain your thinking.

5. Each set of information shows the results of an experiment. The outcomes are the numbers on the cube or the colours on the spinner. They can appear more than once. Study the information. Then copy and complete each drawing to show what the number cube or spinner might have looked like. Explain your reasoning.

a. 100 rolls of a number cube

Outcome	Times Rolled
1	33
2	37
3	30

b. 500 rolls of a number cube

Outcome	Times Rolled
1	260
3	100
5	140

c. 50 spins of a spinner

Outcome	Times Spun
blue	30
green	20

d. 100 spins of a spinner

Outcome	Times Spun
red	33
blue	32
green	35

SKILL BANK
FROM THIS UNIT

1. If you pull out one item at random, describe how likely it is that the item is:
   a. a pair of shorts
   b. a red or white T-shirt
   c. tan or black shorts
   d. a yellow shirt

   If you pull out two items, describe how likely it is that the items are:
   e. tan shorts and a green T-shirt
   f. green shorts and a black T-shirt

2. Draw a spinner for each situation.
   a. more likely to spin an even number than an odd number
   b. certain to spin red or blue
   c. equally likely to spin blue, green, yellow, or red

3. A store offers four flavours of ice cream. List the possible combinations of flavours for double-scooped cones.

4. Design a spinner that has:
   a. three possible unequal outcomes
   b. three possible outcomes that are equally likely

5. A bag contains 6 blue marbles, 9 red marbles, and 12 black marbles. Suppose you pull out one marble. How likely is it that the marble is each colour?
   a. red   **b.** blue   **c.** black   **d.** orange

SKILL BANK
LOOKING BACK

1. Describe the pattern below in numbers. What is the eighth number in the pattern?

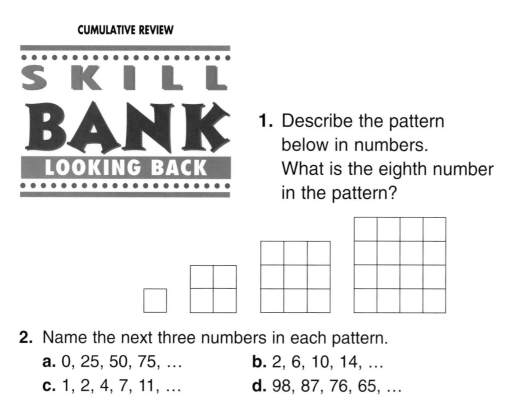

2. Name the next three numbers in each pattern.
   a. 0, 25, 50, 75, …
   b. 2, 6, 10, 14, …
   c. 1, 2, 4, 7, 11, …
   d. 98, 87, 76, 65, …

3. State whether each net will make a pyramid or a prism.

   a.   **b.**   **c.**   **d.**

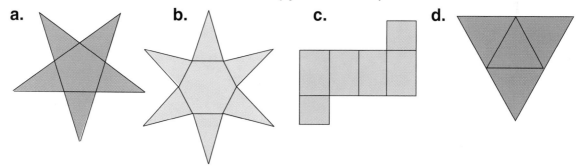

4. Donna made prints of the faces of solids. Name the solid she used for each.

   a.   **b.**   **c.**

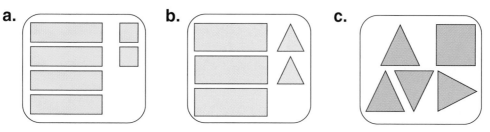

5. Sketch the set of faces for a square pyramid.

6. Draw lines that are:
   a. parallel
   b. not parallel

What should we measure to solve the problem?

1
- What measurements can you find?

- Which measurements tell about how long, how tall, or how far away?

- Which measurements tell about how heavy?

- Which measurements tell about how much liquid?

My Journal: When have you had to measure something to find out how long it is, how heavy it is, or how much liquid it holds?

Words to Know

Length is the distance from one end of an object to the other.

Capacity is the amount of liquid a container will hold.

Mass is how heavy an object is.

RELATING MEASURES

S·T·A·R·T·I·N·G OUT

2 ● For which items might you measure length? What units would you use?

● For which items might you measure capacity? What units would you use?

● For which items might you measure mass? What units would you use?

My Journal: How do you decide which units to use when measuring?

Words to Know

Units of Length	Units of Capacity	Units of Mass
millimetre (mm)	millilitre (mL)	gram (g)
centimetre (cm)	litre (L)	kilogram (kg)
decimetre (dm)		
metre (m)		
kilometre (km)		

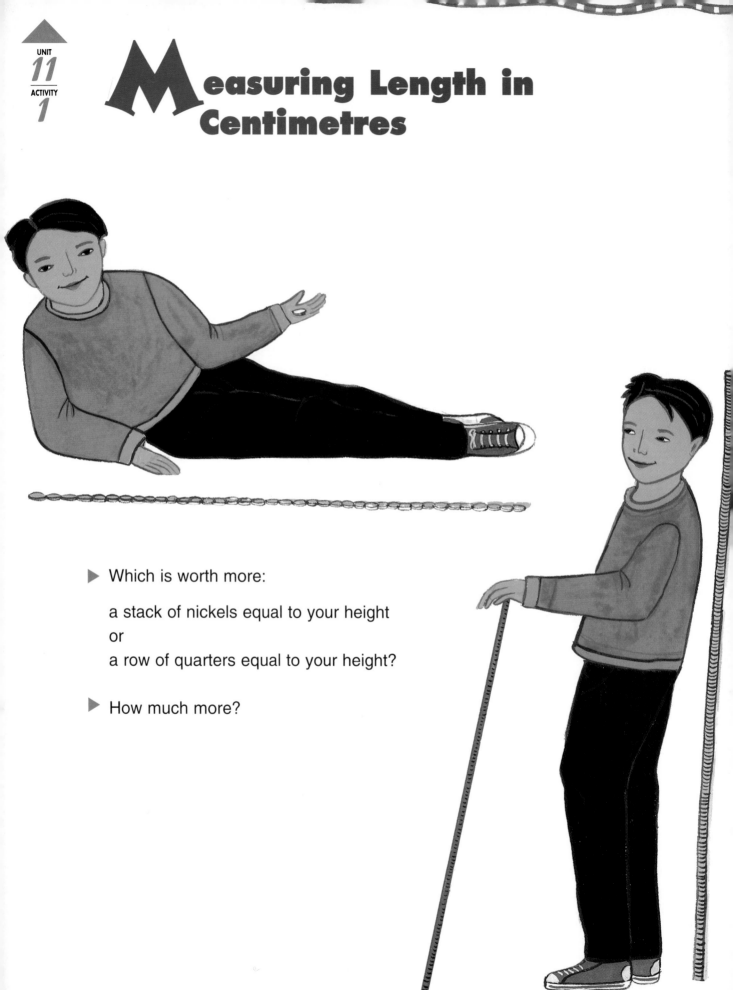

Measuring Length in Centimetres

▶ Which is worth more:

a stack of nickels equal to your height
or
a row of quarters equal to your height?

▶ How much more?

Group

2 players

Materials

Each player needs
- a penny
- a recording sheet like this:

Estimate	Measurement	Difference	Score

- a ruler
- a sheet of paper with
  a starting line drawn
  near the bottom

Rules

① Take turns. The player with the
longer baby finger goes first.

② Put your penny behind the starting
line. Flick the penny lightly. If it
travels off the paper, your turn is
over.

③ Estimate how far your penny
travelled. Record your estimate.

④ Measure and record the actual
distance to tenths of a centimetre.

⑤ Find the difference between your
estimate and your measurement.

⑥ Record your score.

Difference	Points
1 cm or less	3
1 – 2 cm	2
more than 2 cm	1

⑦ The first player to reach 25 points
wins.

Words to Know

centimetre (cm): about the width
of a fingernail
millimetre (mm): about the
thickness of a dime 10 mm = 1 cm

ON YOUR OWN

1. Use six objects, such as a pencil, a toothpick, a paper clip, an eraser, a calculator, and a book. Measure and record the length and width of each object. For each item, explain why you used the units you did.

2. What unit of length would you use to measure each object? Explain your thinking.

   a. the length of a grasshopper

   b. the width of your desk

   c. the thickness of a loonie

   d. the width of a blade of grass

3. Find five objects that you think are less than 30 cm long. Estimate the length of each to the nearest centimetre. Measure it to tenths of a centimetre. Record each measurement in centimetres and in millimetres.

Object	Estimate (cm)	Length (cm)	Length (mm)
paint brush	25	27.6	276

4. *My Journal:* What did you find out about the size of a unit of length and the number of units used to measure?

Practise Your Skills

Draw a line for each length.
1. 10 cm　**2.** 10 mm　**3.** 2.5 cm　**4.** 4.8 cm

5. 50 mm　**6.** 15 cm　**7.** 1.5 cm　**8.** 5.2 cm

Shouting D I S T A N C E

Have you ever wondered how people measured long distances before some of today's tools were invented?

In Egypt, people measured their fields using ropes that were 12 cubits long. A cubit was the distance from an adult's fingertips to elbow. In the desert, people measured the distance between wells by how far away you could hear a shout or how far you could shoot an arrow.

1 How could you compare the distance between your fingertips and elbow to the measurement of a cubit in ancient Egypt? Why do you think it was important to base the measurement on an adult?

2 Explain how accurate you think the method of measuring distance between wells was.

3 Invent any measure of distance you wish. Describe it. What things can you measure with it?

Measuring in Metres

▶ Find five objects in your classroom that you estimate to be close to one metre long or tall.

Estimate the length of each in centimetres.

Then measure each to the nearest centimetre.

Finally, record each measurement as a decimal in metres.

Record your work on a sheet like this:

Object	Estimated Length (cm)	Measured Length (cm)	Measured Length (m)
chair back	80		

Words to Know

centimetre (cm): about the width of a fingernail
decimetre (dm): about the length of a computer disk   10 cm = 1 dm
metre (m): about the height of a door knob   100 cm = 1 m

1. Estimate the length of your stride in metres. Then use that to estimate the length of a room in your home. Write about your work. Describe the room's length using a decimal number.

2. Choose four family members, friends, or neighbours. Suppose they stood side-by-side with their arms stretched out on both sides. Estimate how long that line would be. Write a description of your work.

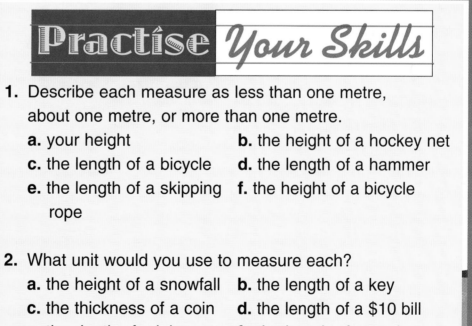

3. *My Journal:* How do decimals help you to report measurements of length?

Practise Your Skills

1. Describe each measure as less than one metre, about one metre, or more than one metre.
   a. your height
   b. the height of a hockey net
   c. the length of a bicycle
   d. the length of a hammer
   e. the length of a skipping rope
   f. the height of a bicycle

2. What unit would you use to measure each?
   a. the height of a snowfall
   b. the length of a key
   c. the thickness of a coin
   d. the length of a $10 bill
   e. the depth of a lake
   f. the length of a pool

Measuring Capacity

UNIT 11 ACTIVITY 4

The tap in the laundry tub is dripping. Carmen noticed that it drips about one drop every second. She put a measuring cup under the tap.
She discovered that 60 drops filled the cup to the 15-mL mark.

▶ If the tap isn't repaired,
how much water will be lost
in one day? How much will be lost in one week?

Words to Know

millilitre (mL):
the amount of
liquid a centimetre
cube would hold

1 cm
1 cm
1 cm

litre (L): 1000 mL = 1 L

274

1. Pick a sandwich that uses mayonnaise. About how many sandwiches could you make with this jar of mayonnaise? Explain your reasoning in writing.

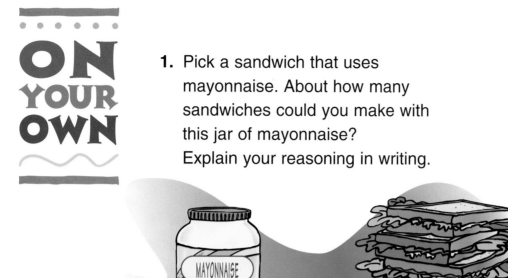

2. *My Journal:* How might the answer to exercise 1 be useful to a chef? Where might a 1 L jar of mayonnaise be used?

Practise Your Skills

1. How many 250 mL cartons of milk would it take to fill the 1 L carton?

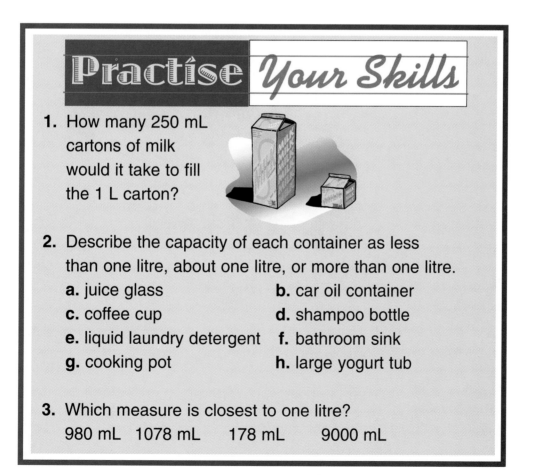

2. Describe the capacity of each container as less than one litre, about one litre, or more than one litre.
   a. juice glass
   b. car oil container
   c. coffee cup
   d. shampoo bottle
   e. liquid laundry detergent
   f. bathroom sink
   g. cooking pot
   h. large yogurt tub

3. Which measure is closest to one litre?
   980 mL   1078 mL   178 mL   9000 mL

 easuring Mass

Suppose you placed pennies side-by-side in a line for one kilometre.

▶ What would the mass of all those pennies be?

Words to Know

gram (g): about the mass of a jelly bean

kilogram (kg): 1000 g = 1 kg

kilometre (km): 1000 m = 1 km

1. Solve the problems below.

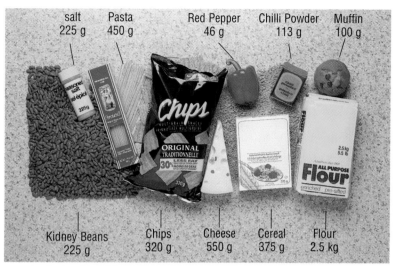

salt 225 g   Pasta 450 g   Red Pepper 46 g   Chilli Powder 113 g   Muffin 100 g

Kidney Beans 225 g   Chips 320 g   Cheese 550 g   Cereal 375 g   Flour 2.5 kg

a. Which product has the greatest mass?

b. Which product has the least mass?

c. Which two products have a total mass of about one kilogram?

d. Which three products have a total mass of about one kilogram?

e. Choose two products. How much heavier is one than the other?

f. Order the products from lightest to heaviest.

2. Explain how you might find the mass of each of these:

a. a goldfish   **b.** a gerbil   **c.** a noodle   **d.** a grain of rice

3. *My Journal:* What is the relationship between grams and kilograms? How do you decide which unit to use when measuring mass?

Practise Your Skills

Order from least to greatest.

1. 600 g,   6.5 kg,   1 kg

2. 2.5 kg,   250 g,   2000 g

3. 1000 g,   3 kg,   1.5 g

The Carrot Caper

- Find out everything you can about your carrot.
- Take as many measurements of it as you can think of.
- Write a description of your carrot that will help someone else pick it out from all the other carrots.

$\mathcal{C}$heck**Y**OURSELF

Great job! Your lost-and-found notice is clear and easy to understand. You included a variety of measurements in your notice and enough detail to enable someone else to find your carrot.

P R O B L E M
BANK

1. Use five empty cans. Estimate which is greater for each can: its height or its distance around. Then estimate the height and distance around for each can. Record your estimates. Measure and record the height and distance around for each can. Compare your findings with your estimates.

2. Use the information about bats on the chart. Answer these questions.

   a. Which bat has the longest wingspan?
   b. Which bat has the shortest wingspan?
   c. Which bats have wingspans of about 0.5 m?
   d. Which bat has a wingspan about four times that of the fruit bat?
   e. How much longer is the wingspan of the false vampire than the mouse-eared bat?
   f. Order the wingspans of the bats from shortest to longest.

BAT DATA	
Name	**Wingspan**
Epomops bat	52 cm
Smoky bat	25 cm
Mouse-eared bat	400 mm
Bismarck flying fox	165 cm
Bumblebee bat	160 mm
Big brown bat	33 cm
False vampire bat	51 cm
Fruit bat	10 cm

3. Charlotte is to make some punch. She will use 1 L of orange juice, 355 mL of ginger ale, and 355 mL of soda water. Can she make the punch in a 2-L jug? Explain your thinking.

4. a. Make lists of products that are sold in containers measuring:
   - less than one litre
   - one litre
   - between one and two litres
   - more than two litres

   b. Explain why some products are sold in smaller containers and some in larger containers.

5. Jolina has three miniature Yorkshire terriers. Peanuts has a mass of 640 g. Popeye has a mass of 1020 g. Buster has a mass of 993 g. Which dog's mass is closest to one kilogram? Explain your thinking.

6. Tony's apples have masses between 150 g and 165 g. About how many apples would it take to make a three-kilogram bag?

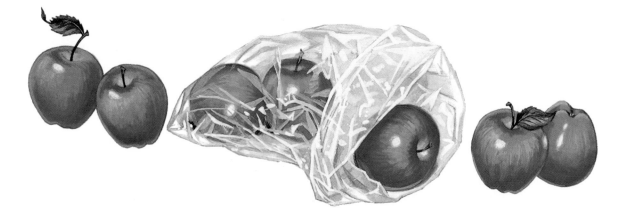

SKILL BANK

FROM THIS UNIT

1. Measure each line.

    a. ─────────────────────

    b. ──────────

    c. ──────

2. Find and list five objects that are

    a. shorter than 10 cm   **b.** longer than 10 cm

3. Choose the best estimate for each measure.

    2 cm   5 cm   12 cm   66 cm   1 m   2 m

    a. the distance around your wrist   **b.** the distance around your finger

    c. the thickness of this math book   **d.** the height of a door

    e. the width of a sidewalk   **f.** the diagonal distance across a TV screen

4. What unit would you use to measure each?

kilograms

centimetres   metres   kilometres   litres

millilitres

    a. the mass of a child   **b.** the length of a necklace

    c. the length of a hallway   **d.** the mass of an apple   grams

    e. the amount of soup in a spoonful   **f.** the distance between cities

    g. the amount of gas in a car

5. Which measure is closest to 5 kg?

    750 g   570 g   5700 g   7500 g

LOOKING BACK

1. **a.** Continue the pattern to the sixth picture.

   x   xx   xxx

          xx   xxx

                 xxx

   b. Write the pattern using numbers.

   c. What would the tenth number be?

2. Write the next three terms in each pattern.

   a. ABA, ABBA, ABBBA …

   b. 18, 24, 30 …

   c. 299, 289, 279 …

   d. 2, 4, 8, 14 …

3. If you roll a number cube labelled 1 to 6 1000 times, about how many times would you expect to roll 3?

4. Design a number cube that would be likely to roll an even number more than half the time.

5. Design a spinner that would be certain to spin an even number.

Index

Acknowledgments

ILLUSTRATION
Cover Illustration: **Seymour Chwast**

Barbara Spurll: 8-9; **Regan Dunnick:** 12-14; **Obadinah Heavner:** 15; **Kevin Hawkes:** 28, 29; **Clarence Porter:** 30-31; **Tadeusz Majewski:** 32-33; **Teco Rodrigues:** 35; **Marc Mongeau:** 36-37; **Brad Gaber:** 46-47; **Joe Lertola:** 48; **Teco Rodrigues:** 52; **Clarence Porter:** 55; **Peter Cook:** 58-59; **Vesna Krstanovich:** 60-61; **Joe Lemonnier:** 63; **Kevin Bapp:** 66; **Teco Rodrigues:** 74; **Mike Shiell:** 80-81, 82-83; **Chris Lam:** 84; **Teco Rodrigues:** 87, 88; **Peter Cook:** 93; **Chris Lam:** 97; **Peter Cook:** 100; **Teco Rodrigues:** 104, 105; **Barbara Spurll:** 110; **Ken Bowser:** 117; **Michael Sours Rohani:** 118-119; **Matt Faulkner:** 121-122; **Clarence Porter:** 125; **Dorothea Sierra:** 126-127; **Barbara Spurll:** 134-135; **Clarence Porter:** 136-137; **Joe Lemonnier:** 138; **Teco Rodrigues:** 139; **Barbara Spurll:** 140; **Ken Bowser:** 142; **Joe Lemonnier:** 143; **Teco Rodrigues:** 144; **Joe Lemonnier:** 147; **Neverne Covington:** 150-151; **Teco Rodrigues:** 152; **Kat Thacker:** 153-154; **Robert Roper:** 158-159; **Tadeusz Majewski:** 163; **Bernadette Lau:** 164; **Vesna Krstanovich:** 168-169; **Joe Lemonnier:** 172; **Cheryl Kirk Noll:** 173; **Margaret Hathaway:** 174; **Kathryn Adams:** 175; **Margaret Hathaway:** 176, 177; **Kathryn Adams:** 181, 191; **Clarence Porter:** 194; **Tomio Nitto:** 200-201; **Peter Cook:** 206-209; **Clarence Porter:** 214-215; **Stephen Harris:** 216-217; **Peter Cook:** 220, 223; **Vesna Krstanovich:** 226-227; **Jerry Dadds:** 228-229; **Jennifer Bolton:** 232-233; **Peter Cook:** 240-241; **Dan Hobbs:** 242-243; **Julia Talcott:** 244-245; **Joe Lemonnier:** 248-249; **Renee Mansfield:** 260; **Norm Eyolfson:** 264-265; **Tadeusz Majewski:** 266-267; **Jackie Besteman:** 268; **Peter Cook:** 270; **Matt Faulkner:** 272; **Teco Rodrigues:** 275; **Bernadette Lau:** 280, 281.

PHOTOGRAPHY
Photo Management and Picture Research: **Omni-Photo Communications, Inc.**

John Lei: 6-7, 15; **Steven Oglivy:** 17; **Ken Karp:** 18; **Spencer Grant/Monkmeyer Press:** 18; **FPG International:** 18; **Renee Sheret/Tony Stone International:** 18; **Frances Anderson/Monkmeyer Press:** 18, 19; **Ray Boudreau:** 20; **Richard Hutchings:** 21; **Claire Aich:** 22-23, 28-29; **Ian Crysler:** 34, 38; © **Eric A Soder/Tom Stack + Associates:** 38-39; **Ian Crysler:** 41, 42-43; **Ken Karp:** 44-45; **Claire Aich:** 50-51; **Richard Pasley/Stock Boston:** 56; **Richard Weiss/Peter Arnold:** 57; **Steven Oglivy:** 62-63; **Tzovaras/Art Resource:** 67; © **Harvey Lloyd/The Stock Market:** 67; © **American Hurrah, NYC:** 71; **Claire Aich:** 72-73; **Ian Crysler:** 78-79, 86, 90-91; **Horizon:** 92; **John Lei:** 95; © **The Stock Market:** 95; **Ian Crysler:** 96, 98, 102-103; **Lowell Georgia/Photo Researchers:** 108; **Danilo Boschung/Leo DeWys:** 108; **Everett Studios:** 108; **Barrie Fanton/Omni-Photo:** 108-109; **Danilo Boschung/Leo DeWys:** 109; **Ian Crysler:** 114, 115; **John Lei:** 114, 115; **Richard Hutchings:** 116; © **The Granger Collection:** 120; **Ian Crysler:** 123; **Everett Studios:** 126-127; **Ian Crysler:** 132-133; **John Lei:** 140; © **D.M. Ratcliffe/Tony Stone Images:** 149; © **Ed Pritchard/Tony Stone Images:** 149; **Ian Crysler:** 160-161, 165, 170, 171, 180; © **Erich Lessing/Art Resource:** 183; **Ian Crysler:** 184, 187-189, 190; **Everett Studios:** 192-193; **Ian Crysler:** 198-199; © **Barrie Rokeach/The Image Bank:** 203; **Ian Crysler:** 205; © **Culver Pictures:** 210; © **Graiton M. Smith/The Image Bank,** © **John Sutton, Photo Search,** © **Wanda Warming/The Image Bank:** 211; **Ian Crysler:** 212-213, 218-219; **Everett Studios:** 224-225; © **Jim Wilson/NYT Picture:** 230; © **Dollarhide/Monkmeyer Press:** 231; **Everett Studios:** 234-235; **Claire Aich:** 238-239; **Steven Oglivy:** 246-247; **Ken Karp:** 251; © **Neal Graham/Omni-Photo Communications:** 251; **John Lei:** 253; **Claire Aich:** 256-257; **Ian Crysler:** 262-263, 271; **Richard Hutchings:** 273; **Ian Crysler:** 274, 276, 277, 278-279.

Permission to reproduce maps on pages 198-199 granted by S.G.A. Limited, Toronto. Maps © S.G.A. Limited.